NAUVOO

The Brigham Young home.

NAUVOO

Photographs by John Telford
Text by Susan Easton Black and Kim C Averett

Deseret Book Company, Salt Lake City, Utah

© 1997 Photographs by John Telford
Text by Susan Easton Black and Kim C Averett

Library of Congress Cataloging-in-Publication Data

Telford, John, 1944–
    Nauvoo / photographs by John Telford : text by Susan Easton Black
and Kim C Averett.
      p.   cm.
    Includes bibliographical references (p.   ) and index.
    ISBN 1-57345-246-7 (hc)
    1. Nauvoo (Ill.)—History.   2. Historic buildings—Illinois—
Nauvoo—Pictorial works.   3. Mormons—Illionois—Nauvoo—History.
I. Black, Susan Easton.   II. Averett, Kim C.   III. Title.
F549.N37T45   1997
977.3'43—dc21   97-9846
                                                       CIP

Printed in Hong Kong by Palace Press International

10 9 8 7 6 5 4 3 2 1   68875

CONTENTS

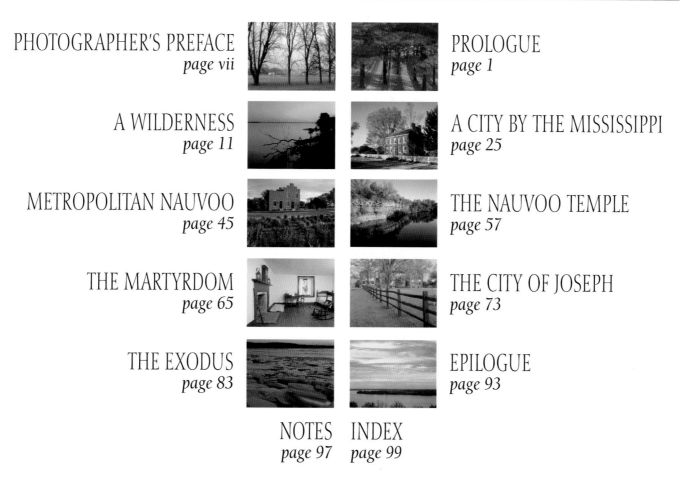

Sarah Granger Kimball home seen through the trees on a winter morning.

PHOTOGRAPHER'S PREFACE

Before the spring of 1995, Nauvoo was a place that I had only heard or read about as related to the history of The Church of Jesus Christ of Latter-day Saints. I had heard stories of the city and the Saints who lived there, and of their forced exodus across the Mississippi River as they began their legendary trek to the Salt Lake Valley. But I had never been there. My sister and her husband, Cindy and Kim Averett, who were living in Lincoln, Nebraska, frequently described the beauty of Nauvoo and the spirit that pervades this important Church historic site. Cindy kept saying to me, "We ought to do a book on Nauvoo."

I had been on the faculty of Brigham Young University for four years at that time. Having stood in awe of the creative work that several of my talented colleagues had done to support the Church, I made a commitment to myself to follow their example. A grant proposal through my college, Fine Arts and Communications, was accepted, which would allow me one week in Nauvoo to produce enough photographs, both interior and exterior, to compile a book. With excited anticipation I called Kim and Cindy to set the date. We decided

on the third week of May, when trees and flowers should be in bloom but before the heat and humidity of summer.

And then a sense of panic came over me. Every other

book I had done took years of work in the field. How could I possibly get all the photographs I needed in six days? Would the light and weather cooperate? Could we get permission and cooperation from the authorities in Nauvoo? I had never even been to Nauvoo—how would I find the time to scout the sites, do all the extensive set-up and lighting for each interior photograph, and on and on? Yet I felt a sense of peace and purpose about the project.

A full moon rose into a purple sky over the Mississippi as we crossed the bridge approaching Nauvoo on the Sunday night that would begin our week's work. Valerie, my wife, and I were traveling with Kim Averett, my brother-in-law, co-author, and guide. Just reading the billboard announcing "Nauvoo, one mile" sent chills of anticipation down my spine. "This is it," I thought. "This is where Joseph lived. This is where the Saints built the beautiful city."

It was dark, but the full moon shed enough light to illuminate places that we had previously known only in stories. The Homestead, Brigham Young's home, Heber C. Kimball's home, and Parley Street running right into

Joseph's Creek, named in memory of Joseph Smith.

the Mississippi River each brought a flood of emotion. I had heard the stories, and now I was standing right where they had occurred. Here was Joseph. Here was Brigham. The Twelve and the Saints whose accounts I knew only from words on a page had been here.

I kept waking up during that first night and walking to the window of the motel to see if the moon was still in a clear sky. I nervously tried to visualize where it would be at sunrise. Finally, when the agreed-upon predawn hour arrived, the three of us got up, knelt in prayer, and set out to begin the long-anticipated photographic work.

The moon was still bright in a sky that was beginning to take on hues of pink and purple. Experience had taught me that we had less than twenty minutes to find the place, set up the camera, calculate the settings, and make the exposure. After looking at two or three possibilities, we decided on the Seventies Hall. Using the longest lens I had (450mm) to keep the moon as large as possible in relation to the building, we set up in a field of dewy wet grass for the first of more than one hundred photographs. Click, two seconds at f.45, the first transparency was exposed. And we moved on.

We photographed each morning beginning about five-thirty, shooting until the "sweet light" around sunrise faded into ordinary daylight, and then turned our attention to interior photographs. We worked inside until late afternoon, when the light was favorable for

Flowers bloom along the fence of the Sarah Granger Kimball home.

Joseph Smith's Red Brick Store.

outside work again, then photographed outside until after sunset—nine or nine-thirty—and went home to prepare for the next day.

The third morning was overcast and rather ominous looking. Disappointment started to set in as I said to myself, "We have only six days to do all this work; I need every morning to be clear and beautiful." But I went out anyway to see what might present itself. The dramatic sky hanging over the Heber C. Kimball home

moved me, and I made two exposures. Later that same day it started to rain—hard. While we were doing the interior photographs of the Wilford Woodruff home, the rain was pounding outside. Before it was through, four inches of rain had fallen.

The next morning we were tempted to sleep in. But again I thought, "We have been presented with these conditions; let's go see what we can make of them." As we drove halfheartedly past the Red Brick Store, I felt

compelled to get out of the car and take a look. I found myself walking into the trees, farther and farther away from Joseph's store, trying to step around the puddles that had collected from the previous night's rain. Then I turned around to see a scene of unexpected beauty: the reflection of the store in one of the largest pools of rainwater. During the week, several other picture opportunities presented themselves as I found myself being drawn to vantage points that were not typical for me,

Red water pump behind the Joseph Coolidge home.

and I realized that my prayers for guidance were being answered. In addition, the variety of weather provided much more diversity in one week than we ever could have hoped for.

Then, of course, there was the chance meeting with Susan and Harvey Black. Over dinner in the home of William Weeks (the architect of the Nauvoo Temple), we talked about how we were all working on prospective books about Nauvoo. By the end of dinner we were all pretty much working on the same book.

Because of the success of the one week in May, my college grant was renewed, making it possible for me to return to Nauvoo three more times during different seasons. The last of those trips fell on the weekend of February 1–4, 1996, the sesquicentennial commemoration of the Saints' exodus from Nauvoo. Temperatures had dropped to the subzero equivalent of what they had been 150 years before. In spite of the cold, I felt comfortable in a Nauvoo that was now familiar to me. As we drove to Montrose, Iowa, to participate in the lighting of the commemorative bonfire, a full moon was rising into a cold winter sky over the frozen Mississippi. It was a familiar friend in a place that is now full of friends.

Several people need to be acknowledged for their help and contributions to this book. Elder James Sorensen, director of Nauvoo Restoration, Inc., graciously accepted our proposal to make the photographs in Nauvoo. Carol Hill, NRI administrative assistant, patiently allowed us to work in the interiors of many of the Nauvoo buildings, including moving furnishings and other objects for the best picture opportunities. Elder Grant Fry, who succeeded Elder Sorensen as NRI director, also provided continued support for the making of the photographs. Brother and Sister Bill and Sid Price, public affairs missionaries, have been a great help and support in all of our work, along with the many missionary couples who cooperated so fully with us in the making of the interior photographs. We gratefully acknowledge the permission and cooperation given to us by Roger Yarrington and Don Albro to photograph the sites that are owned by the Reorganized Church of Jesus Christ of Latter Day Saints. And, of course, without the vision and support of Sheri Dew, vice president of publishing at Deseret Book, along with the talents of Kent Ware and Emily Watts, this book would not have been possible. This has been an unusual team effort that has involved the creative effort of several people. I must also acknowledge what a privilege it has been to work with Kim Averett and Susan Easton Black. Their knowledge about Nauvoo is endless, and the difficulty of deciding what to include in a limited number of pages was handled with grace and cooperation. In spite of the numerous comments and suggestions for change, there was never a single word of disagreement or threatened ego. It has been a beautiful experience from beginning to end.

John Telford

Sandy, Utah

Trees on the Mississippi shoreline at the north end of Nauvoo's Main Street.

The sun's rays shine through the pines in the Nauvoo State Park.

PROLOGUE

In nineteenth-century western New York, contending religious revivalists claimed to represent Jesus Christ. Young Joseph Smith, confused by their contradicting Christian doctrines, sought clarity through prayer. The divine answer he received and the vision he saw of "two Personages, whose brightness and glory defy all description," filled his soul with eternal truth.[1] The sharing of that truth in his small community of Palmyra, New York, led to open contempt and mockery of the young boy by his neighbors.

Rather than succumb to the harassment, Joseph declared: "I had actually seen a light, and in the midst of that light I saw two Personages, and they did in reality speak to me. I knew it, and I knew that God knew it, and I could not deny it."[2]

Three and a half years after Joseph's first divine manifestation, Moroni, an ancient prophet who had lived in the Americas in A.D. 400, appeared as a resurrected being to him. The angel told the seventeen-year-old boy about some sacred engravings "written upon gold plates giving an account of the former inhabitants of this continent."[3] In 1829 Joseph Smith, by the gift and power of

God, translated the ancient writings, which became known as the Book of Mormon—Another Testament of Jesus Christ.

The book was shared with family, friends, and seekers of truth from the farthest frontiers of the United States to the British Isles. "From the first time I read this volume of volumes, even till now," penned convert William W. Phelps, "I have been struck with a kind of

sacred joy at its title page. . . . What a wonderful volume! What a glorious treasure! By that book I learned the right way to God; by that book I received the fulness of the everlasting gospel; . . . and I was made glad."[4]

Convert George Cannon stated, "No wicked man could write such a book as this; and no good man would write it, unless it were true and he were commanded of God to do so."[5]

As believers embraced the truths of the Book of Mormon, disbelievers shunned their choice and rallied in angry mobs to overthrow what they perceived as the evil encroachment of Mormonism upon contemporary Christianity. "Hell may pour forth its rage like the burning lava of Mount Vesuvius, or of Etna," declared Joseph Smith, "yet shall 'Mormonism' stand. . . . Truth is 'Mormonism.' God is the author of it."[6]

Joseph's firm testimony made him a target of persecution and mobocracy. The believers who testified that he was a prophet also suffered. When the father of Joseph Smith was told to "burn up those Books of Mormon" in order to be forgiven "the whole debt" of a small delinquent note, Father Smith refused, knowing

Stand of trees on Nauvoo's Mississippi shoreline.

that his refusal would mean his imprisonment. "I was not the first man who had been imprisoned for the truth's sake," he thought, "and when I should meet Paul in the Paradise of God, I could tell him that I, too, had been in bonds for the Gospel which he had preached."[7]

When Mother Smith was accosted by a Presbyterian pastor who said, "And you are the mother of that poor, foolish, silly boy, Joe Smith, who pretended to translate the Book of Mormon," Lucy was unruffled. "Why do you apply to him such epithets as those?" she asked. The reverend scoffed, "Because he should imagine he was going to break down all other churches with that simple 'Mormon' book." Lucy countered, "Let me tell you boldly, that the book contains the everlasting gospel. . . . Mark my words—as true as God lives, before three years [Mormonism] will have more than one-third of your church."[8] The minister's hearty laugh diminished when Elder Jared Carter baptized a third of his congregation.

Hyrum Smith also defended the truths his younger brother Joseph espoused. "I had been abused and thrust into a dungeon, and confined for months on account of my faith, and the testimony of Jesus Christ," wrote Hyrum. "However I thank God that I felt a determination to die, rather than deny the things which my eyes had seen, which my hands had handled, and which I had borne testimony to."[9]

Unswerving conviction characterized thousands of converts to The Church of Jesus Christ of Latter-day Saints amid their trials in the 1830s in New York, Ohio, and Missouri. Even though they were the objects of mockery and persecution, they did not deny their beliefs or the truth of their religion. With resolute faithfulness they followed their prophet-leader Joseph Smith in pioneering communities and establishing schools on the western frontier. At great personal sacrifice they constructed

The moon sets over the Seventies Hall.

Day dawns on the Mississippi River.

Brigham Young's home (left) and the Seventies Hall can be seen through the maple trees.

a temple, a House of the Lord, in Kirtland, Ohio, contrary to the predictions of jeering critics.

The greatest trial to their faith was a state-sanctioned extermination order issued by the governor of Missouri in 1838. In the winter of 1838–39, men, women, and children were forcefully driven from their Missouri homes because of the extermination order. They trekked across the state and forded the icy Mississippi River seeking safety. One refugee, Parley P. Pratt, recalled his first reaction upon reaching Illinois: "I immediately stepped a few paces into the woods, and, kneeling down, kissed the ground as a land of liberty, and then poured out my soul in thanks to God."[10]

Residents of the small town of Quincy, Illinois, welcomed the exiled Latter-day Saints. Quincy lawyer O. H. Browning exclaimed: "Great God! have I not seen it? Yes, my eyes have beheld the blood-stained traces of innocent women and children, in the drear winter, who had traveled hundreds of miles barefoot, through frost and snow, to seek a refuge from their savage pursuers."[11] He and other town leaders advised the citizenry "to be careful not to say anything calculated to wound the feelings of the strangers thrown into their midst."[12] The local Democratic Association resolved that the exiles were "entitled to our sympathy and kindest regard, and that we recommend to the citizens of Quincy to extend all the kindness in their power to bestow on the persons who are in affliction."[13]

The Saints were grateful for the outpouring of kindness they received in Quincy, but longed for a home of their own, a city in which to worship God in peace. Near an unlikely bluff overlooking a bend in the Mississippi River, their longings would be fulfilled, but not without

A glimpse through a grove in Nauvoo reveals homes built by early Latter-day Saints.

additional suffering and sacrifice. In just six years they would create from the marshy lowlands a beautiful city—Nauvoo.

Although Elder Heber C. Kimball helped drain the swampland, build homes, cultivate farms, and set up shops in the fledgling community, the Spirit whispered to him that Nauvoo would be only a temporary refuge. Church leader Sidney Rigdon was enraged at Heber's pessimistic view and denounced his colleague by stating, "I should suppose that Elder Kimball has passed through sufferings and privations and mobbings and drivings enough to learn to prophesy good concerning Israel."[14]

However, Heber was correct. As it turned out, Nauvoo was only a stopping point, a refuge from the storm for the Saints. "We were . . . glad of a resting place out of the reach of those who had sought our lives," wrote Sarah Rich. "We were truly a thankful and humble people."[15]

By the early 1840s, old settlers along the Mississippi and riverboat passengers were applauding Nauvoo as the "Jewel of the Mississippi." J. H. Buckingham, a gentleman from Boston, wrote: "No one can visit Nauvoo, and come away without a conviction that . . . the body of the Mormons were an industrious, hard-working, and frugal people. In the history of the whole world there cannot be found such another instance of so rapid a rise of a city out of the wilderness—a city so well built, a territory so well cultivated."[16]

Visitors and converts daily swelled the population of the emerging community. They often sought audience with the town's leading citizen, Joseph Smith. "I have had the pleasure of welcoming about one hundred brethren [today]," wrote the Prophet. Among those he greeted was English convert Jane Robinson, who mused: "It was a

The frozen Mississippi River at the end of Nauvoo's Parley Street.

This rocking horse, belonging to John Taylor's son, was carried from Nauvoo to the Salt Lake Valley. It was recently returned to the John Taylor home in Nauvoo.

severe trial to me, in my feelings to leave my native land and the pleasing associations that I had formed there; but my heart was fixed. I knew in whom I had trusted and with the fire of Israel's God burning in my bosom, I forsook my home."[17] Another convert, a young woman of African descent, Jane Manning, wrote that in order to reach Nauvoo, she and her family had "walked until our shoes were worn out, and our feet became sore and cracked open and bled until you could see the whole print of our feet with blood on the ground."[18]

Joseph Smith welcomed so many converts and visitors to Nauvoo that one onlooker suggested, "You must do as [Napoleon] Bonaparte did—have a little table, just large enough for the victuals you want yourself." The Prophet's wife, Emma Smith, replied, "Mr. Smith is a bigger man than Bonaparte: he can never eat without his friends."[19]

One of the most distinguished Nauvoo visitors was Josiah Quincy, a former mayor of Boston. He wrote of Joseph Smith: "It is by no means improbable that some future textbook . . . will contain a question something like this: What historical American of the nineteenth century has exerted the most powerful influence upon the destinies of his countrymen? And it is by no means impossible that the answer to the interrogatory may be thus written: Joseph Smith, the Mormon Prophet."[20]

That is our conviction. Within these pages you will learn of Joseph Smith and the city he orchestrated and called Nauvoo. You will read of the Prophet's love for his followers, and learn of Nauvoo as it struggled to reach sacred heights and then, in a brief moment of jealous avarice and plunder, fell to obscurity. The saga of Nauvoo and its architect, the Prophet Joseph Smith, needs to be told, though it may never be fully understood.

Window in the Pendleton Schoolhouse.

A winter sunrise near the Joseph Smith Homestead. The Homestead was one of two block houses built before the Saints settled near the bend in the Mississippi River.

The Mississippi River at sunrise.

A WILDERNESS

In the 1830s, marshlands bordering the Mississippi River were touted as a bargain by entrepreneurs to unsuspecting investors in the East. Land speculation in frontier "paper towns" of Illinois was considered an investment windfall for fortunate buyers. Speculators like Isaac Galland, Horace Hotchkiss, and James White led the list of those who saw the potential for a quick dollar in an infested swamp known first as Quashaquema by the Sac and Fox Indian tribes, then as Venus in 1834, and by 1839 as the "paper town" of Commerce.

Captain James White, the first permanent Caucasian settler in the area, exchanged two hundred bags of corn with the Indians for the swamp. He shuffled his land holdings within a network of speculators, expecting to profit from an unwarranted bonanza. But his optimism was crushed by the financial panic of 1837 and 1839. Because Commerce was only an unreclaimed marsh, about 185 miles north of St. Louis and 250 miles south of Chicago, there seemed little hope it would ever be profitable.

The panic, coupled with negative rumors of the

remote location, left little basis for speculators' projections of growth. Where could the entrepreneurs find buyers for their investment gone sour? When none came forward, the speculators offered to sell Commerce in 1839 for almost no money down.

The Latter-day Saint exiles from Missouri were enticed by the offer and could afford little more. Among their number was Israel Barlow, who had fled from the horrors of the extermination order to the Des Moines River, where he was found by local settlers. His account of cruelties against the Saints evoked the tender sympathies of the Iowans. Iowa's territorial governor, Robert Lucas, encouraged the "citizens in their humane and benevolent exertions to relieve this distressed people, who are now wandering in our neighborhood without comfortable food, raiment, or a shelter from the pelting storm."[1]

The Iowans not only supplied Barlow with personal clothing and food but, more important to the founding of Nauvoo, gave him an introductory letter to land speculator Isaac Galland. Galland immediately recognized the magnitude of the Mormon influx in the area and

Sunset across the river.

The Homestead was Joseph Smith's first dwelling in Nauvoo. The block-house portion was built before he arrived in the vicinity. The small log cabin was used as a summer kitchen.

seized the opportunity to exchange his swamp in Illinois for valuable Missouri landholdings abandoned by the Latter-day Saints.

The Prophet Joseph Smith said of the swamp: "The place was literally a wilderness. The land was mostly covered with trees and bushes, and much of it was so wet that it was with the utmost difficulty that a footman could get through, and totally impossible for teams."[2] He further observed, "Commerce was unhealthy, very few could live there; but believing that it might become a healthy place by the blessing of heaven to the saints, and no more eligible place presenting itself, I considered it wisdom to make an attempt to build up a city."[3]

On 24 April 1839, Joseph Smith "advised the brethren, who could do so, to go to Commerce and locate in Dr. Galland's neighborhood," which consisted of "one stone house, three frame houses, and two block houses, which constituted the whole city of Commerce."[4] The Prophet resided in one of the block houses, known as the Homestead. However, he soon moved into a tent to make room for a few of the sick to reside in his home. Many settlers were dying from the epidemic diseases in the area. "It was a very sickly time," wrote Wilford Woodruff. "The large number of Saints who had been driven out of Missouri were flocking into Commerce, but had no homes to go to."[5] Weakened by their ordeals and living in makeshift tents

Interior of the original portion of the Homestead.

and wagons, thousands of Saints fell prey to the illnesses of the Mississippi Valley.

Elizabeth Ann Whitney described her family as "all sick with ague, chills, and fever, and [we] were only just barely able to crawl around and wait upon each other."[6] Zina Jacobs lamented: "Disease continues to prey upon the children. O Lord how long shall we labor under these things, even children suffering so sore? Wilt thou hasten the time in thine own way when the Saints shall have power over the destroyer of our mortal body."[7] Nearly eighteen hundred people were buried on the bluffs overlooking the Mississippi River in the Nauvoo Burial Grounds. Death from malaria and the strange fever reached such heights in 1841 that coffin makers struggled to keep up with the demand.

To thwart the spread of disease, a plan was devised to dig large ditches to drain the swampland in Commerce. Since the clay and limestone layers beneath the topsoil prevented the water from being absorbed, it was hoped that the drainage ditches would alleviate the problems inherent in the marshy flatland. Reverend George Peck observed the Latter-day Saints digging the ditches and noted with surprise: "Some 200 miles above St. Louis, we saw on the Illinois side of the river a very singular encampment. A multitude of people, men, women, and children, ragged, dirty, and miserable generally, seemed to be living in tents and covered wagons for lack of better habitations. This strange scene presented itself

The statue depicts a pioneer family laying a child to rest in the Old Nauvoo Burial Grounds. It was sculpted by Dee Jay Bawden and Richard D. Young in 1989.

Headstones dating to the Latter-day Saint era are still prominent in the Old Nauvoo Burial Grounds.

along the shore for a mile or more. We were informed that they were Mormons, who had recently fled from Missouri."[8]

Although disheartened by the herculean efforts required to drain the swamp, the Saints did not quit. As Joseph Smith observed the tenacity of his followers, he renamed the small village *Nauvoo,* a Hebrew word meaning "beautiful place or situation." He believed that a community of Saints would rise on the remnants of the swamp and become a "light of the world—a city set upon a hill."[9] So confident was he in his hope for the future city that he commissioned the Twelve Apostles to bring converts from the four corners of the earth to Nauvoo.

As Wilford Woodruff departed on a mission to share the news of the restored gospel with those in the British Isles, he became ill and looked "more like a subject for the dissecting room than a missionary."[10] Others of the Twelve left sickly families. When Heber C. Kimball bid farewell to his wife, she was "shaking with a chill, having two children lying sick by her side." He recorded: "My inmost parts would melt within me at leaving my family in such a condition, as it was, almost in the arms of death. I felt I could not endure it." His companion, Brigham Young, had similar feelings upon leaving his wife and children. Their farewell shout of "Hurrah, hurrah, hurrah for Israel!" evoked a "Good-bye; God bless you!" from loved ones.[11]

Water from the bluffs above Nauvoo collected in the flatlands to form a swampy bog. The Saints dug trenches to drain the bog; a stone arch is built over the main trench in Nauvoo.

The kitchen and dining area of the Homestead was built by Joseph Smith. The area was used as the administrative office of the Church for several months.

The Pendleton Schoolhouse consists of a two-level block house, where the family lived, and a lean-to connected to the back, where school was held.

The apostles and their families were not alone in suffering from the prevailing illnesses in the swamp. Benjamin Brown recorded: "Numbers of the sick and dying had to lie on the ground, with only a blanket over them. . . . It was frequently declared that the persecutions in Missouri were small matters compared to the miseries endured at this period in Nauvoo."[12] His son, Lorenzo Brown, lamented his personal ten months of suffering, "I do not recollect having a good night sleep during the time."[13] Mosiah Hancock penned: "Sometimes my parents were so ill they could hardly move, and I would take a quart cup and fill it with water from the spring that was about 60 yards from the house. Then I, being weak, would crawl on my arms and knees, and place the cup of water ahead of me and crawl to it each time I reached it, until I reached the house."[14]

With illness and death on every side, Joseph Smith questioned whether he would also succumb. He sought the answer from his father, Joseph Smith Sr. "You shall even live to finish your work," his father promised him. Joseph cried out, "Oh! my father, shall I?" "Yes," said his father, "you shall live to lay out the plan of all the work which God has given you to do."[15]

Part of that plan was to build Nauvoo as a chartered community consisting of 3,733 acres, then the largest city in the state of Illinois. The proposed charter, passed by the Illinois legislature and signed into law in February 1841, gave control of the election process and

The Jonathan Browning family lived in this block house before their brick home and gun shop were built.

the municipal court system to the city's residents. It guaranteed them the right to establish a university and a military legion. Joseph Smith was jubilant over the self-governing guarantees of the Nauvoo Charter. He scoffed at critics who jeered when he told the people he would build the city. "The old inhabitants replied 'We will be damned if you can.' So I prophesied that I would build up a city, and the inhabitants prophesied that I could not."[16]

The unconquerable spirit of the Saints truly made Nauvoo the "city beautiful." They drained the wetlands and constructed shelters for hundreds and later thousands who gathered there. They transformed the low-lying peninsula from an undesirable swamp into a thriving community. The chief architect of the transformation was the Prophet Joseph Smith. He designated the land to be plotted true north, with streets running at right angles to the survey line. The four-acre-square blocks between the streets were equally divided into one-acre lots. Flower gardens, orchards, fences, and out-buildings such as barns, stables, summer kitchens, and smokehouses were encouraged. The Saints followed their prophet's plan for Nauvoo, even though working the marshy soil extracted a heavy toll. "The soil differs much from anything I ever saw," wrote Sarah Scott. "The mud here sticks to my feet just like paste."[17]

Transforming the Illinois swamp into Nauvoo, a scene of "singular and most striking beauty," required

A windowpane in the Jonathan Browning block house shows the wavy imperfections of period glass.

Sparse furnishings in the Browning block house demonstrate the austerity of many early Saints.

the cooperative efforts of all the followers of Joseph Smith.[18] The city did not begin with quaint, stately looking brick homes and shops. The first homes in Nauvoo, called "block houses," were constructed of hewn logs. These differed from "log cabins"; the cut and squared timbers were laid on top of each other and the spaces between them "chinked," or filled with mud and clay. The leader of the emerging community wrote of the houses in 1840, "The Saints have already erected about two hundred and fifty houses at Nauvoo, mostly block houses, a few framed, and many more are in course of construction."[19] A few years later Thomas Gregg, an Illinois newspaperman, reported that Nauvoo had about "1200 hand-hewn cabins."[20]

The Saints took pride in their crude dwellings, often whitewashing them to give them a distinctive New England look. Resident Abigail Pitkin wrote of her home:

> In Nauvoo City we reside,
> Where we in peace can now abide,
> Our dwelling measures "Thirteen Feet,"
> With walls rough-hewn and white-washed neat.
> Our bed springs up against the wall
> Because our room is rather small;
> For we in building count the cost
> Lest too much money should be lost.[21]

Heber C. Kimball, returning from his missionary labors in England, noted how Nauvoo had grown in his

absence: "When we got in sight of Nauvoo [coming up the Mississippi by riverboat] we were surprised to see what improvements had been made since we left home. You know there were not more than thirty buildings in the city when we left about two years ago, but at this time there are 1200; and hundreds of others in progress which will be finished."[22] It is estimated that from 1839 to 1846 the inhabitants of Nauvoo cleared thirty thousand acres and built twelve hundred block houses, five hundred wooden homes, and more than three hundred brick structures. The settlers originated from nearly every state in the Union and a few foreign countries. Nearly one-third spoke with an English accent. German-speaking converts joined with Norwegian and Afro-American believers to build and beautify Nauvoo. Sawmills, brickyards, kilns, and gristmills were commonplace.

Each builder left a legacy, an enduring imprint on the town. It was the lives of the Saints that made Nauvoo the city beautiful, as much as the homes they built. Colonel Thomas L. Kane observed their handiwork: "A beautiful city lay glittering in the fresh morning sun. . . . The city appeared to cover several miles, and beyond it, in the background, there rolled off a fair country, checkered by the careful lines of fruitful husbandry. The unmistakable marks of industry, enterprise, and educated wealth everywhere, made the scene one of singular and most striking beauty."[23]

The rough-hewn timbers of the Pendleton Schoolhouse show how block houses were constructed.

The Pendleton Schoolhouse in winter.

Wilford Woodruff counted and handpicked the 14,574 bricks used in his home.

A CITY BY THE MISSISSIPPI

The Latter-day Saints tackled the temporary housing problem in Nauvoo with the same zeal that characterized their efforts to reclaim the swamp. With hammer, saw, trowel, and shovel, they replaced the squalor of makeshift tents and log cottages with the beauty and stability of more permanent structures. Although complaints were few, journal entries like the following evidence dissatisfaction with the temporary quarters. "The house we lived in . . . was little more than a shelter," penned Eliza Gibbs. "It was clapboarded on the outside but not plastered inside, and the clapboards were so old and warped that we could stick our hands through between the boards all around the sides of the house."[1]

The sights and sounds of bustling Nauvoo seemed epic to passersby, many of whom marveled at the refined changes in the shantytown. "Nauvoo grew, with magic rapidity, from a few rude homes to a magnificent city," wrote journalist Harvey Cluff. "Houses increased in number, farms were opened up and prairie lands east of the city converted into prosperous fields of golden grain."[2] To John Butler it appeared that "everyone was building and you could look over the little settlement

and see the hand of industry in every corner of the town. It began to be a more healthy country and folks began to be strong again . . . thanks be to God, our Heavenly Father, . . . it yielded and brought forth in abundance."[3]

Almost forgotten were the earlier days of Nauvoo, when coping with starvation and learning to survive had been paramount to daily existence. Journal entries of extreme deprivation, such as "flour was hard to get" and "I only [had] corn meal for bread" and "about out of flour" were scarce by 1842.[4] John Butler's diary account of his family living on "crabapples and honey for nine weeks and nothing else to eat only what game we could kill once in a while" was unusual.[5]

Cornmeal was now almost erased from the daily diet, whereas it had often been the main course of breakfast, lunch, and dinner in 1839. Joseph Smith's prayer of thanks for "this johnnycake" (a cooked mixture of water, cornmeal, and molasses) and his request for "something better" was treated as a remembrance of yesteryear, sparking gratitude for better times as recipes for applesauce and "Admiral Peacock's pickle for meat" were exchanged.[6] Also shared through the *Nauvoo Neighbor* newspaper were better ways to succeed at daily chores: "If you would obtain all the milk from the cow you must treat her with the utmost gentleness, she must not stand trembling under your blows nor under

Bustle oven on the exterior of the Lucy Mack Smith home.

The parlor of the Wilford Woodruff home. The rocking bench has spots for both mother and sleeping baby.

Wilford Woodruff's parlor features his-and-her rocking chairs. Elder Woodruff took the hatbox-trunk on his mission to England.

During the Christmas season, the Mansion House was festively decorated.

your threats. She may at times need a little chastise-ment, but at such times you need not expect all her milk."[7]

To further encourage the Saints' success, Joseph Smith authorized the formation of the Big Field Association for community planting to promote self-sufficiency. The 3,800 acres in the field east of Nauvoo were divided into six sections and used for public plant-ing and consumption. The first harvest from the Big Field was a boon to Nauvoo settlers: "Thirty thousand bushels of corn, nearly the same amount of wheat" were harvested. John Taylor stated that the Field also yielded an "abundance of oats, barley, buckwheat, potatoes and other vegetables." To him the bountiful harvest proved, "God helps them that help themselves."[8]

Visitor Josiah Quincy stated that the Field and the town were "magnificently laid out, and teeming with activity and enterprise." Of the town architect, Joseph Smith, Quincy observed, "Born in the lowest ranks of poverty, without book-learning, and with the homliest of all human names, he had made himself . . . a power upon earth . . . [and] had won the hearts and shaped human lives."[9]

The Prophet's reaction to such praise was humility, coupled with a desire to give greater service. "My house has been a home and resting-place for thousands, and my family many times obliged to do without food, after having fed all they had to visitors," said Joseph Smith.

When the Prophet moved his family into the Mansion House in 1842, the study area of the home became the administrative office for the Church.

The Lucy Mack Smith home.

Still, he lamented that he could not do more for the Saints. His move from the crowded Homestead to the Mansion House did little to relieve his costs. "I have been reduced to the necessity of opening 'the Mansion' as a hotel," he wrote.[10]

One Latter-day Saint, observing Joseph Smith doing "woman's work" in the Mansion House to relieve the burdens of his wife, concluded that mismanagement by Emma was the root of the domestic problems. "I said to him, Brother Joseph, my wife does more hard work than does your wife." Joseph replied, "If a man cannot learn in this life to appreciate a wife and do his duty by her, in properly taking care of her, he need not expect to be given one in the hereafter." The judgmental advisor meekly concluded: "His words shut my mouth as tight as a clam. I took them as terrible reproof. After that I tried to do better by the good wife I had and tried to lighten her labors."[11]

As Joseph and Emma Smith graciously welcomed the poor and the acclaimed to the Mansion House, the Saints busily worked to build their own homes so they too could host new arrivals. Nauvoo teemed with building activity. Home and shop next to barn and stable, with a family garden in between, quickly became the norm. Yet there was nothing normal about the growth of the city. Almost overnight Nauvoo became recognized as a boomtown bordering the Mississippi River. The laziness of the meandering river was in sharp

John Taylor's home was between the Times and Seasons *and Nauvoo Neighbor* Printing Office *and the post office.*

contrast to the grist and lumber mills, potteries, tanneries, brickyards, bakeries, and dozens of other home industries springing up all around.

The mere fact that the Latter-day Saints were succeeding on a swamp when contemporaries in advantaged eastern cities were destitute was surprising, if not frustrating, to the critical visitor. "Sadly . . . was I disappointed," wrote the Reverend Samuel Prior after his visit to Nauvoo. "Instead of seeing a few miserable log cabins and mud hovels, which I had expected to find, I was surprised to see one of the most romantic places that I have visited in the West. The buildings, though many of them were small and of wood, yet bore the marks of neatness which I have not seen equalled in this country."[12]

Those who had once mocked the Saints were surprised by the refined architectural style of the dwellings, which reflected not only the owners' preferences but their places of origin: New Englanders built federal-style homes, while New Yorkers patterned their houses after the Greek revival style. Home construction was financed on what outsiders considered a shaky exchange system. Even the gullible knew that bartering for services and goods, letters of credit, and informal IOUs spelled financial disaster for community building. Yet piano lessons, education, and even the services of midwives were exchanged for food and clothing in Nauvoo.

The Heber C. Kimball home in evening light.

For the Saints, building a city on trust, mutual respect, and common purpose proved their only viable chance to succeed.

Although the houses were simple in design, there was nothing simple about the process of creating a sturdy, permanent dwelling. For example, making bricks began as four parts of clay were mixed with one part sand and just enough water to make "brick dough." The dough was then shaped in molds greased with lard and tallow. Damp bricks were dried for three weeks, being carefully turned each day to ensure uniform drying. Once dry, the bricks were fired for six to eight days in kilns heated to 2100 degrees Fahrenheit. It took thirty-three days from the mixing pond to the kiln before a single brick was ready to be sold for a half-cent. With the average two-story dwelling requiring forty thousand bricks, the cost of such an edifice was unthinkable for many, but ultimately more than 350 brick buildings were constructed in Nauvoo.

Brigham Young was among the fortunate few to build a brick home. "Although I had to spend the principal part of my time at the call of Brother Joseph in the service of the Church," he wrote, "the portion of time left me I spent in draining, fencing, and cultivating my lot . . . and otherwise finishing my home." On 31 May 1843 he reported, "I moved out of my log cabin into my new brick house, . . . and felt thankful to God for the privilege of having a comfortable though small habitation."[13]

An elevated root-cellar entrance was built next to Brigham Young's home. The triple-wall construction of the cellar kept the interior temperature near 55 degrees F. year-round.

Living room of the Heber C. Kimball home.

The Heber C. Kimball home boasted an ornate widow's perch.

A wintry day did not hamper the work of the gunsmiths at the Jonathan Browning home and gun shop.

One of the most beautiful brick structures was owned by Heber C. Kimball. It boasted an intricate Flemish pattern of bricklaying and a picturesque circular arch of oversized bricks. Heber expressed much joy when his home was completed "both inside and out."[14]

The prolific diarist Wilford Woodruff wrote on 22 May 1843, "Several of the brethren proffer to assist me to brick and other materials and help me put it into a house." Wilford worked alongside the laborers day after day, sorting the bricks and selecting the best ones for the front wall. On 3 May 1844 he wrote, "I hung four doors primed them and laid my lower floors," and the next day he recorded, "I moved in to my new brick house."[15]

The industry and sacrifice needed to build better homes and farms were seen again and again in neighborhoods throughout Nauvoo. Wilford Woodruff wrote of his impression of the John Benbow farm: "His farm looked almost like a Garden of Eden. I have never seen more work done in one year on a prairie farm than was done on his."[16] Once farms were cultivated and homes built, the settlers needed outlets or shops in which to sell their wares and work their trades. Combining home and shop proved successful for gunsmith, tinsmith, shoemaker, and baker alike.

Attached to the Jonathan Browning home was the shop where the famed gunsmith challenged the notion, "the longer the gun barrel, the more accurate the gun." It took two weeks of work to shape the metal and to

A muzzle-loaded, black-powder gun and powder horn near the mantle in the Jonathan Browning home.

form each "lock, stock and barrel." Jonathan then sold the gun—with his trademark inscribed on the catchbox, "Holiness to the Lord, our Preservation"—for twenty-four dollars.

Sylvester Stoddard built a tin shop onto his home. With smoldering irons, flanges, and other tools he could make a pan in twenty minutes and sell it for ten cents. He was a versatile tinsmith, making cookie cutters for the bakers, candle safes for the candle makers, and pudding steamers for the English converts. His most successful product was the cast-iron stove.

George Riser had his shoe shop in the family kitchen. He competed with twelve other cobblers in Nauvoo and even a pharmacy that advertised shoes for sale.[17] It took from seven to eight hours for Riser to make a pair of custom shoes, using cowhide, wooden pegs, lasting tacks, and rawhide. When the pair of shoes was finished it sold for less than two dollars.

The Lucius Scovil family lived in a log cabin on the back of their property on Main Street and built a brick bakery on the front section. They competed in the bakery business by advertising "Marriage cakes made to order on the shortest notice from one to twenty-five dollars each."[18] To gain a competitive edge over the four other bakers in town, Lucius built a bustle oven to maximize the use of heat. In the oven he cooked breads, pies, cookies, cakes, and crackers to tantalize his customers.

Sylvester Stoddard made his wares in the tin shop adjoining his home.

The Lucius Scovil Bakery was a favorite of those wanting baked goods in Nauvoo. The summer kitchen is at the left rear of the building.

The New England clapboard-style home of Joseph Coolidge served as a hotel and cooper shop.

Joseph Coolidge opened barrel-making, candle-making, and pottery businesses in his colonial-style home. In the wet cooper's shop he made three barrels a day and sold each for twenty-five cents. In the candle shop family members unraveled cotton clothing to create tie strings, weighted the strings with rocks, and dipped them in animal fat or beeswax to form candles. His most expensive candles were dipped thirty times, and he personally guaranteed them to burn for twenty-four hours. In the pottery shop family members and employees crafted pots that were used everywhere from the barn to the dining room.

The artisan, the craftsman, and the merchant of Nauvoo enjoyed prosperity for a season. Such competitive advertisements as "will sell cheaper than the cheapest" kept prices within range of most consumers.[19] Merchant Amos Davis made notations in a day book of his prices and those who trafficked with him: "Hyrum Smith 1 pair boys shoes $1.34 . . . James Mulholland 15 lbs. Nails $1.87 . . . Vinson Knight 1 axe $2.25, 3 molasses $.56, pepper $.25, paper $1.83, candle $3.72 . . . Newell Knight 1 broom $.31, 1 bed chord $.37."[20]

Fearful that customers might be lured to the Davis General Store, Windsor Lyon advertised in the *Nauvoo Neighbor*, "Received, by Steamers . . . a splendid stock . . . Dry Goods, Groceries, Crockery . . . Books and Stationery, Drugs and Medicines, Paints and Dye stuffs, Boots, Shoes, Military Goods; . . . Those wishing to

A variety of merchandise was sold at the Windsor Lyon Drug and Variety Store.

make good investments with their money will do well to call at Lyons' cheap cash store."[21] Not to be outdone by his competitors, Parley P. Pratt publicized "NEW GOODS, VERY CHEAP . . . just received from Boston the largest supply of Dry Goods ever opened in this city, . . . Cash wanted, and country produce bought and sold. . . . As we intend selling goods very cheap, . . . no one need ask for credit, nor waste breath in bantering on the price."[22]

One English convert appreciated the mercantile competition: "Meat is cheap, two pence (four cents) a pound of choice pieces, one pence a pound [for] the other, fowls, one shilling (twenty-five cents) eggs two pence (four cents) a dozen. . . . Vegetables are high," she wrote, but added her plan for the future, "We hope by next year to grow our own."[23]

Thus by 1843 the Latter-day Saints had tamed a swamp, reclaimed a wilderness, and built a progressive city from the flats to the bluffs. Craftsmen, artisans, and skilled laborers had created a legendary community that was spoken of with envy as the "Jewel of the Mississippi." Hyrum Smith explained why the community building had been and would continue to be so successful: "The gospel picks out all the big souls, out of all creation; and we will get all the big souls out of all the nations, and we shall have the largest city in the world."[24]

Several brick kilns in Nauvoo fired the thousands of bricks that were used in the construction of homes, stores, and other buildings.

The Cheap Riser Boot Shop was one of several shoe stores in Nauvoo.

The proprietor of the Windsor Lyon Drug and Variety Store boasted of his fresh herb garden, plants from which were used in medicinal remedies.

METROPOLITAN NAUVOO

As immigrants swelled the population of Nauvoo, diverse social and ethnic interests found expression in the metropolitan city. Southerners brought refinement, Northerners introduced the Protestant work ethic, and British converts brought the hope that the status of "ladies and gentlemen" was possible for every man and woman in Nauvoo. As the diverse Saints carved their niches in Nauvoo society, they sought for cultural expression. Music, theater, dancing, parades, and the arts found ready audiences.

The townsfolk needed relief from the riveting chores involved in transforming the Illinois wilderness into a city; a cultural event was a welcome change. Perhaps they thought a good night on the town would cure what ailed them. If not, the herbologist merchant-healer was ready with unsolicited advice and remedies that could kill or cure.

A sign outside the Windsor Lyon Drug and Variety Store depicted a lion symbolically roaring about his healing wares. The proprietor invited prospective customers in with the advertisement that his store offered an unspecified "thousand other articles too numerous

to mention."[1] Most of the medicinal wares were produced in a garden behind his shop: lobelia, hollyhocks, sassafras, and skunk cabbage, common ingredients in a pharmacist's prescription.

Lyon's botanical remedies were a mixture of home-grown herbs, folklore, and charm. His remedy for the common cold was: "conserve hollyhock take one pound fresh blossoms and add four pounds white sugar and pound into a paste. Take two ounces of poplar bark, one

ounce of cayenne and so forth and make a thick dough."[2] For twenty dollars his customers could buy *A New Guide to Health,* read of other imaginative remedies, and become certified to practice Thompsonian medicine. Knowing of the inherent weaknesses of the prescribed remedies, many residents hoped that a momentary diversion—a play, dance, or musical event—was all they really needed.

Any celebration was an opportunity for the Saints to escape from the daily routine and forget about their ills. They paused from their chores to celebrate Independence Day, for example, watching military processions and listening to patriotic speeches and brass bands. Given the heritage of government persecution against their people, often the military band, rather than the speeches, was the highlight of the patriotic event. On Independence Day 1842, Native Americans and spectators from neighboring cities and villages joined with the Saints in celebrating the nation's freedom. The final festivity of that day featured "Mrs. Emma Smith and the ladies of other distinguished officers [accompanying] their companions on the parade."[3]

Home-grown herbs were a staple ingredient in nineteenth-century medicine.

Whether parade, dance, or choir concert, an event requiring music was never the perfect occasion unless William Pitt's Brass Band played. One member, Charles Hales, wrote of playing with the band at "every public festival. . . . We played for the Nauvoo Legion, the dedication of the 70's hall, and for the laying of the capstone of the Lord's house."[4]

With music as the paramount focus of cultural refinement in Nauvoo, it seemed natural that a Music Hall be erected north of the Nauvoo Temple grounds. Musical productions filled the Hall to overflowing even though some of the performances lasted nearly five hours. An editorial describing one musical event reads: "I would ask where are we to go for music, if we do not find it in Nauvoo? I will boldly assert, nowhere. Witness the concert the other evening . . . got up for the most laudable and praiseworthy purpose. The music in its selection was of the most varied character, and the electrifying feeling that was manifest proved to demonstrate that Nauvoo can furnish us with ladies and gentlemen whose instrumental and vocal powers are of no unpolished order."[5]

Joseph Smith recognized dancing as another needed diversion from the everyday hardships. The merry strains of the violin and the caller's voice moved dancers through the quadrilles, Scotch-reels, and French-fours. As one dance neared its close, John Taylor stated that all who attended "felt mutually edified and blessed" by

The Seventies Hall, cleared of pews, is festive with Victorian Christmas decorations.

The Wilford Woodruff home is decorated in a traditional German style for Christmas.

The John Taylor home at Christmastime.

joining in the merriment.[6] The Saints' leaders were reported to be agile on the dance floor, with the exception of Parley P. Pratt. Orson Hyde "observed brother Parley standing in the figure, . . . making no motion particularly, only up and down. Says I, 'Brother Parley, why don't you move forward?' Says he, 'When I think which way I am going, I forget the step; and when I think of the step, I forget which way to go.'"[7]

Often those who joined in the dance also enjoyed theater, drama, and related arts. They read with eagerness the poet's words that memorialized events and people in rhyme:

> O tell me not of Ancient Rome,
> of Athens, or of Troy;
> Gone, gone is all their greatness
> without one gleam of joy,
> Nor speak ye yet more modern names,
> tho fair and lovely too;
> What is their beauty, what their fame,
> compared to fair Nauvoo?[8]

For the "young at heart," a circus or a riverboat excursion opened a vista of cultural wonder, a window to the world. Many enjoyed greeting the "exploration parties and tourists up and down the river admiring the grandeur of the scenery and magnificence of the temple and city."[9] But the favorite activity of river watchers was welcoming returning missionaries and new arrivals to town. Heber C. Kimball wrote, "We landed in Nauvoo on the 1st of July (1841), and when we struck the dock

Inside the John Taylor home, traditional English Christmas decorations are featured.

I think there were about three hundred Saints there to meet us, and a greater manifestation of love and gladness I never saw before."[10]

The Cultural Hall or community center was the hub of Nauvoo's nightlife. In the Hall farmers and craftsmen enjoyed dances, banquets, and theatrical productions. The first stage play presented there was *Pizzaro*, starring none other than Brigham Young. He once observed: "If I were placed on a cannibal island and given a task of civilizing its people, I should straightway build a theatre. . . . On the stage of a theatre can be represented in character evil and its consequences, good and its happy results and rewards, the weaknesses and follies of man and the magnanimity of the virtuous life."[11]

For those wishing to pursue academics, classes were offered by professors Orson Pratt and Orson Spencer at the University of Nauvoo. A town lending library boasted two hundred volumes on science, world religion, history, and literature. For the fundamental courses of reading, writing, and arithmetic, small schoolrooms welcomed students throughout the community. Music instruction was also available, as evidenced by English convert Ann Pitchforth's advertisement, "Piano-Forte Music . . . wishing to suit the circumstance of the Saints . . . Reference, kindly permitted, to Elders Brigham Young and John Taylor."[12]

A favorite activity among the brethren was participating in lyceums and debate societies. Discussions

The Cultural Hall was the activity center of Nauvoo.

Traditional prairie-style Christmas decorations are displayed in the Pendleton Schoolhouse. The cookies were made with period cookie cutters.

The Sylvester Stoddard home and tin shop is festive for the holidays with its traditional Scottish Christmas decorations.

Santa visits the Stoddard home and tin shop in his horse-drawn sleigh.

from the religious to the political stimulated even the sleepy farmer to take a stubborn, opinionated stance. Topics of debate ranged from "Ought capital punishment to be abolished?" to "Should females be educated to the same extent as males?" to "Is there sufficient evidence in the works of nature to prove the existence of a God?"[13]

For those who enjoyed the clever quips found in autograph books, Brigham Young's lines provided a wry smile:

> To live with Saints in Heaven is bliss and glory,
> To live with Saints on Earth is another story. [14]

The favorite cultural occasion was always a party. Hosea Stout wrote of a birthday party he attended: "I went; we had a most agreeable entertainment and had a very delicious supper. . . . I have been to but few such agreeable parties in my life. . . . All seemed of one heart and partook of the enjoyment of the good things and comforts. . . . May they all have many more such good and happy nights."[15]

Perhaps the most unforgettable parties were hosted at the Mansion House. The party commemorating Joseph and Emma Smith's fifteenth wedding anniversary began at ten o'clock in the morning. "Conversation continued on various topics until two o'clock, when twenty-one sat down to the dinner-table, and Emma and myself waited on them," wrote the Prophet.[16] The party didn't end until favorite songs were sung.

Lights flickered inside the Printing Office during early dawn hours as editors scurried to make last-minute changes in the newspaper.

The biggest parties of the year were held on Christmas Day. Throughout Nauvoo, family members and friends visited each other's homes in progressive-dinner fashion, sang favorite yuletide songs, and danced. For Joseph and Emma Smith, the Christmas of 1843 was especially memorable. They invited more than fifty couples to the Mansion House for a gala event. The guests began arriving at 2:00 P.M. and ate a sumptuous dinner before stepping onto the dance floor. That evening a man with hair "falling over his shoulders, and apparently drunk," purporting to be a Missourian, disturbed the festivities. Upset by the intrusion, Joseph summoned the police to escort the man from his home. During the ensuing scuffle the Prophet recognized the intruder as "my long-tried, warm, but cruelly persecuted friend, Orrin Porter Rockwell," who had recently escaped from a Missouri prison.[17] Joseph embraced his friend and celebrated his merriment with gusto that Christmas Day.

Nauvoo was a vibrant, metropolitan city. The diverse cultural, social, and ethnic interests filled the community with music, theater, dancing, parades, and the arts. A sophistication thought possible only in the eastern states or Europe became vital to the community life of Nauvoo. It was more than just a diversion from the struggle to reclaim the Mississippi River swampland or a "good night" in a new frontier town. It was an artistic expression of all that was "of good report, or praiseworthy."[18]

Inside the Printing Office a "galley" of the Nauvoo Neighbor *is prepared for printing using hand-set type.*

Stones from the limestone quarry near the Mississippi River were hewn and then shaped to create the exterior facade of the Nauvoo Temple.

THE NAUVOO TEMPLE

The temple Joseph Smith envisioned for Nauvoo was larger and more magnificent than the one the Saints had built in Kirtland, Ohio.[1] Upon completion it would be the largest building north of St. Louis and west of Chicago in the Mississippi Valley. "I am not capacitated to build according to the world," the Prophet told the *Pittsburgh Gazette* editor. "I know nothing about architecture and all that."[2] Yet he had definite ideas about how the Nauvoo Temple should be constructed. To architect William Weeks he said: "I wish you to carry out my designs. I have seen in vision the splendid appearance of that building illuminated, and will have it built according to the pattern shown me."[3] That pattern called for a three-story, gray-limestone structure measuring 128 feet in length and 88 feet in width. Ornamental crescent moonstones, sunstones, and five-pointed starstones were to be carved in the exterior of the structure to adorn thirty pilasters. A belfry and a clock tower dome with a gilded weather vane would top the building.

Structural renderings clarifying Joseph Smith's vision of the temple were drawn by William Weeks. Once the renderings were approved by the Prophet, Weeks was given authority to proceed with the building phase without interference. As he perfected his pen-and-ink sketches, the Prophet approved his designs for circular stairways, starstones, round windows, a baptismal font, sunstones, and some interior decorations.

Rather than wait for final temple plans, workers began quarrying limestone near the Mississippi River almost the day the temple was announced. Saints volunteered one day in ten to cut and haul limestone blocks to the temple site. Laboring in the quarry was fraught with danger, as men operated hand drills and placed black gunpowder in the holes they bored. They blasted out large chunks of limestone, which fell to the ravine below. Tons of stone were retrieved from the ravine and pushed and pulled to the temple site to be polished.

One of the men who helped haul stones to the site was Brother Bybee. One day, after he had "hitched his team to his wagon and with his son had gone to the quarry to load a large stone into the wagon, . . . their wagon became stuck in a mud hole." Joseph Smith "waded into the mud [to help dislodge the wagon] . . . the wagon moved a bit, and the horses were able to keep it going." Brother Bybee called out, "Thank you, Brother Joseph." His son was impressed that the Prophet "was not above wading in mud halfway to his knees and getting his shoulder covered with mud to help another man in distress."[4]

Luman Shurtliff also worked in the quarries. "We labored ten hours a day, and got something to take to our families for supper and breakfast," he wrote. "Many times we got nothing; at other times we got a half pound of butter or three pounds of fish, beef, and nothing to cook it with. Sometimes we got a peck of cornmeal or a few records of flour . . . or anything we could get to sustain us . . . and thank God that I and my family were thus blessed. . . . I have seen those that cut stone by the year eat nothing but parched or browned corn for breakfast and take some in their pockets for their dinner and go to work singing the songs of Zion. I mention this not to find fault or to complain, but to let my children know how the temple of Nauvoo was built, and how their parents as well as hundreds of others suffered

to lay a foundation on which they could build and be accepted of God. . . . We would rather live poor and keep the commandments of God in building a temple than to live better and be rejected with our dead."[5]

While men like Bybee and Shurtliff blasted limestone from the quarries, other men traveled by riverboat to the Wisconsin pineries to cut lumber for the temple. The timber was floated downriver, forming large rafts that covered nearly an acre and "contained one hundred thousand feet of sawed lumber and sixteen thousand cubic feet, or one hundred ninety-two thousand square feet, of hewn lumber."[6]

As the men worked to construct the Nauvoo Temple, the women sought ways they might also help. "Through the sanction and permission of Hyrum Smith and the Prophet and others," Mary Fielding Smith and her sister Mercy Thompson began a penny fund to buy nails and glass for the temple.[7] Women in each Nauvoo neighborhood contributed spare pennies to the fund. To Eliza R. Snow it seemed that "every talent and exertion [were] peculiarly needed for the erection of the Temple," and every Latter-day Saint in Nauvoo was expected to tithe in labor, goods, and money for its completion.[8] Goods such as meats, poultry, eggs, clothing, furniture, and family heirlooms were donated as tithing. Drusilla Hendricks wrote of paying "a good deal of tithing by making gloves and mittens."[9]

Sarah Kimball gave perhaps the most unusual donation.

The miniature Nauvoo Temple replica shows in detail the craftsmanship and artistic talents of the temple builders.

Sunstones were placed atop each of the thirty pilasters that formed the exterior walls of the Nauvoo Temple.

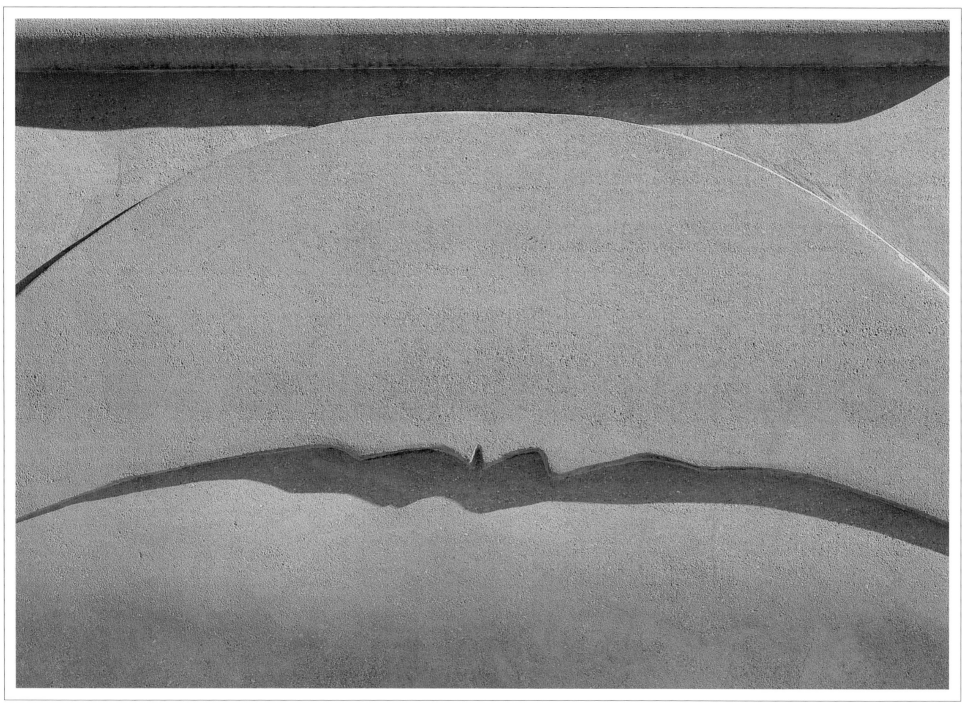

A contemporary replica of a moonstone can be seen at the Nauvoo Temple site.

"My husband came to my bedside," she recalled after the birth of their son, "and as he was admiring our three-day-old darling, I said, 'What is the boy worth?'" Her husband, Hiram Kimball, replied, "Oh, I don't know; he is worth a great deal." Sarah suggested the sum of one thousand dollars and he agreed. She then announced to her non-Mormon husband that her half of their son, five hundred dollars, would be donated to the Nauvoo Temple fund. When Hiram Kimball related the incident to Joseph Smith, the Prophet replied, "I accept all such donations, and from this day the boy shall stand recorded, Church property."[10] The Prophet gave Hiram the option of giving the boy to him as trustee-in-trust or paying the money to the Nauvoo Temple fund. Kimball gave a city block to the Church.

In the spring of 1844 Wandle Mace wrote, "Joseph suggested the propriety of putting all the forces upon the temple, . . . until the temple was completed, for said he, 'we need the temple more than anything else.'"[11] William W. Phelps penned in verse the importance of the endeavor:

> Go carry glad tidings, that all may attend,
> While God is unfolding "the time of the end";
> And say to all nations, whatever you do,
> Come, build up the Temple of God at Nauvoo.

> So say to the great men, who boast of a name;
> To kings and their nobles, all born unto fame,
> Come, bring on your treasures, antiquities, too,
> And honor the Temple of God at Nauvoo.[12]

This plate is inscribed, "Mormon Temple, Nauvoo Illinois, 1841–1845—Potter, J[oseph] Twigg, Kilnhurst Old Pottery, England, 1839–1866." Only two Nauvoo Temple plates exist in Nauvoo today.

The Saints willingly gave of their time and means to build the Nauvoo Temple. Joining in that effort was the Prophet Joseph Smith. However, his physical exertion of pushing and pulling the limestone into place was often interrupted when a laborer requested, "Brother Joseph, talk to us." A gospel conversation would soon ensue. "I could lean back and listen. Ah what pleasure this gave me," wrote Wandle Mace. "[The Prophet] would unravel the scriptures and explain doctrine as no other man could. What had been mystery he made so plain it was no longer mystery."[13] Brigham Young added, "[Joseph] took heaven, figuratively speaking, and brought it down to earth; and he took the earth, brought it up, and opened up, in plainness and simplicity, the things of God."[14]

During those gospel conversations, Joseph Smith explained the covenants made and ordinances performed in holy temples. He assured his followers that through participating in temple ordinances they would become more committed to a Christlike life and have a greater love for God. He taught, "The pleasing joys of family ties and associations contribute to the happiness, power and dominion of those who attain to the celestial glory."[15] Mace wrote, "I ask, who understood anything about these things until Joseph being inspired from on high touched the key and unlocked the door of these mysteries of the kingdom."[16]

Though the construction of the Nauvoo Temple was an edifying labor of love, its economic cost drained the resources of the emerging community. "Some say it is better to give to the poor than build the Temple," remarked Joseph Smith. He countered, "The building of the Temple has sustained the poor who were driven from Missouri, and kept them from starving; and it has been the best means of this object which could be devised."[17] To console those who felt the economic hardship, the Prophet promised, "[They] shall have the first claim to receive their endowments in the temple."[18]

Encouraged by his promise, the Saints worked harder and sacrificed their personal comforts to build the Nauvoo Temple. Their sacrifice was duly noted, but what brought acclaim from friend and foe alike was the unique edifice they constructed. Jacob Scott penned, "The Temple exceeds in splendor and magnificence any building I have ever seen."[19] Another visitor noted, "It was a large and splendid edifice, built on the Egyptian style of architecture, and its grandeur and magnificence truly astonished me."[20] Typical of newspaper tributes was an editorial that appeared in the *New York Sun*: "The building of the Mormon Temple under all the troubles by which those people have been surrounded, seems to be carried on with a religious enthusiasm which reminds us of olden times."[21]

The southeast cornerstone of the Nauvoo Temple was designated the First Presidency Corner. The baptismal font was in the center of the temple, which is at the lowest depression in the ground.

In the bricked area near the northwest cornerstone of the Nauvoo Temple was a grand circular staircase.

On the afternoon of 27 June 1844, Joseph Smith, his brother Hyrum, Willard Richards, and John Taylor occupied this room.

THE MARTYRDOM

The peaceful existence of the Latter-day Saints in Nauvoo was threatened in the winter of 1843–44. Neighboring communities became jealous of the emerging city and its growing prosperity. Feeding off the jealous resentment, community leaders in nearby Warsaw and Carthage threatened violence against the Saints residing in Nauvoo if they would not abandon their holdings and leave Illinois. Ridicule and evil speaking were the weapons used to rally the mob element prevalent in the surrounding areas. Thomas Sharp, editor of the *Warsaw Signal,* predicted, "War and extermination is inevitable!" against the Saints of Nauvoo. He encouraged those residing in Warsaw and Carthage to take up arms and destroy the city: "CITIZENS ARISE, ONE AND ALL!!! Can you stand by, and suffer such INFERNAL DEVILS! to rob men of their property and RIGHTS, without avenging them. We have no time for comment; every man will make his own. LET IT BE MADE WITH POWDER AND BALL!!!"[1]

The inevitable target of the proposed extermination was the prophet-leader and mayor of Nauvoo, Joseph Smith. "Joe Smith is not safe out of Nauvoo," trumpeted

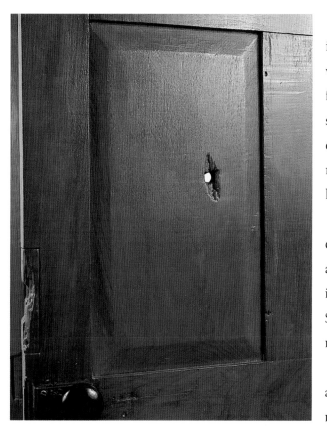

the *Warsaw Signal.* "We would not be surprised to hear of his death by violent means in a short time. He has deadly enemies. . . . The feeling of this country is now lashed to its utmost pitch, and will break forth in fury upon the slightest provocation."[2]

Despite the publicized threat of murder, Nauvoo's leading citizen was calm. "God Almighty is my shield; and what can man do if God is my friend? I shall not be sacrificed until my time comes; then I shall be offered freely," said Joseph Smith. Some time later, he told the Saints: "I do not regard my own life. I am ready to be offered a sacrifice for this people; for what can our enemies do? Only kill the body, and their power is then at an end."[3]

The Prophet did attempt to escape from the threat of death by fleeing from Nauvoo to the Iowa Territory. Ill-advised friends encouraged him to return and face an illegal arraignment in Carthage. With resignation Joseph Smith said, "If my life is of no value to my friends it is of none to myself."[4] He returned to Nauvoo.

Early on Monday morning, 24 June 1844, the Prophet and his brother Hyrum left Nauvoo on their final journey to Carthage. As Joseph Smith gazed upon the city he had orchestrated, he said, "This is the loveliest place and the best people under the heavens; little do they know the trials that await them." To friend Dan Jones he confessed, "I love the city of Nauvoo too well to save my life at your expense. If I go not to them, they will come and

The door of the Carthage Jail room where Joseph and Hyrum Smith were killed bears holes from mobbers' bullets.

act out the horrid Missouri scenes in Nauvoo. I may prevent it. I fear not death. My work is well nigh done. Keep the faith and I will die for Nauvoo."[5]

For Joseph and Hyrum Smith, Carthage was a scene of broken promises, conspiracy oaths, illegal arraignment, and incarceration. "Could my brother Hyrum but be liberated," Joseph mused, "it would not matter so much about me."[6] Around five in the afternoon of 27 June 1844 "an armed mob—painted black—of from 150 to 200 persons" surrounded the Carthage Jail, where the brothers were imprisoned, and began shooting.[7] Hyrum was the first to die; a bullet shot by a mobber struck him on the left side of the nose. His last words were, "I am a dead man!" Bending over the body of his lifeless brother, Joseph sobbed, "Oh dear, brother Hyrum!"[8]

The next to fall from the assassins' bullets was Joseph Smith. He was struck by two bullets fired from the doorway and two fired from outside the jail. His final words were, "O Lord my God."[9] He then fell from the window of the upper story of the Carthage Jail to the ground below.

When news of the martyrdom of Joseph and Hyrum Smith reached Nauvoo, the citizens bitterly mourned the death of their leaders. "Yea, every heart is filled with sorrow, and the very streets of Nauvoo seem to mourn. Where it will end the Lord only knows," wrote Vilate Kimball.[10] Eliza R. Snow expressed the Saints' anguish in verse:

The Carthage Jail was constructed of limestone in 1824. In 1844 only two rooms were used to retain prisoners; the jailer and his family resided in the remaining rooms.

The bodies of Joseph and Hyrum were secretly buried in the courtyard of the partially completed Nauvoo House.

Oh Illinois, thy soul has drunk the blood,
Of prophets martyred for the Cause of God.
Now Zion mourns—she mourns an earthly head.
The Prophet and the Patriarch are dead.[11]

The grief of Newel Knight was poignantly written: "O how I loved those men, and rejoiced under their teachings! It seems as if all is gone, and as if my heart strings will break, and were it not for my beloved wife and dear children I feel as if I have nothing to live for."[12]

On 28 June 1844 the bodies of the martyrs were brought from Carthage to Nauvoo. Their widows, Emma Smith and Mary Fielding Smith, were among the first to view their remains in the Mansion House. "Yea I witnessed their tears, and groans, which was enough to rent the heart of an adamant," lamented Vilate Kimball. "Every brother and sister that witnessed the scene felt deeply to sympathize with them."[13]

Even as the widows and the citizens of Nauvoo mourned the loss of their leaders, public declarations were announcing the end of Mormonism. The editor of the *New York Herald* quipped: "The death of the modern mahomet [sic] will seal the fate of Mormonism. They cannot get another Joe Smith. The holy city must tumble into ruins, and the 'latter day saints' have indeed come to the latter day."[14] But such a bold dismissal of the Church was premature.

Illinois governor Thomas Ford testified, "The murder

"In life they were not divided, and in death they were not separated" (D&C 135:3). This statue of Joseph and Hyrum was sculpted by Dee Jay Bawden.

This beautiful, ornate chest, owned by Emma Smith, contains a false bottom in which the manuscript pages for Joseph Smith's translation of the Bible were hidden.

of the Smiths, instead of putting an end to [Mormonism] only bound them together closer than ever, . . . [giving] them new confidence in their faith."[15] Orson Hyde prophesied: "Instead of the work dying, it will be like the mustard stock that was ripe, that a man undertook to throw out of his garden, and scattered seed all over it, and next year it was nothing but mustard. It will be so by shedding the blood of the Prophets—it will make ten saints where there is one now."[16]

The increase of the Latter-day Saint population in Nauvoo was dramatic after the martyrdom. To many it did seem that where there had been one Saint, there were now ten on the streets of the city. Neither anti-Mormon sentiment nor even the death of the Prophet seemed to deter the influx of new converts; they came from England, Scotland, Canada, and the United States to make Nauvoo their home. The constant tide of immigrants swelled the population of the city and increased prosperity. The fame of Nauvoo soon reached beyond the Mississippi River.

The mushrooming community angered the neighboring mob element even further. Mobbers had hoped that the deaths of Joseph and Hyrum Smith would end Mormonism in Nauvoo and that the prosperity of the city would subside. But their hopes were ill founded, for Nauvoo had yet to reach its potential.

The bodies of the martyrs were brought back to the Mansion House from Carthage on 28 June 1844.

The bodies of the martyrs have been exhumed and reinterred three different times. The current grave site of Joseph, Hyrum, and Emma Smith is in a family cemetery adjacent to the Homestead.

The Printing Office, post office, and John Taylor home on Main Street were a natural hub of activity in 1845 as news of the completion of the Nauvoo Temple and of the exodus was announced.

THE CITY OF JOSEPH

As anti-Mormon sentiment escalated, rumors of impending violence increased. Recognizing the mob mentality in the neighboring communities, Governor Thomas Ford advised Latter-day Saint leaders: "It would be good policy for your people to move to some far distant country. Your religion is new and it surprises the people as any great novelty in religion generally does. . . . I do not foresee the time when you will be permitted to enjoy quiet."[1]

Outraged Saints decried the governor's suggestion of an exodus. A poem of the period conveys the frustration many felt about the threat of exile:

> The mobocrats have done their best,
> Old Sharp and Williams with the rest.
> They've burnt our houses and our goods
> And left our sick folk in the woods.
>
> Below Nauvoo on the green plains,
> They burnt our houses and our grains.
> And if they fought, they were hell bent
> To raise for help the government.
>
> Old Governor Ford, his mind so small,
> He's got no room for soul at all.
> If heaven and hell should do their best,
> He neither could be damned nor blessed.[2]

As a few fearful Saints trembled under the specter of persecution, others threatened to disrupt the peace of citizens in Warsaw and Carthage. The Quorum of the Twelve Apostles—the leading council of the Church after the death of Joseph Smith—attempted to curb the feelings of the fearful and militant by assuring them that they would not be removed from their city and that their community would yet be "a stronghold of industry and wealth."[3] Members of the Quorum of the Twelve believed Nauvoo would still prosper and become a memorial to Joseph Smith, even "The City of Joseph." William W. Phelps supported the unifying counsel of these leaders against the relentless rumors of exile: "We have hitherto walked by sight, and if a man wanted to know anything he had only to go to Brother Joseph. Joseph has gone, but he has not left us comfortless. . . . If you want to do right, uphold the Twelve."[4]

The City of Joseph did grow in wealth and numbers as never before. George A. Smith wrote: "An immense immigration [into the city] is expected this Spring, and notwithstanding the departure of apostates and their followers from our city, it is almost impossible to find an empty house or a room to rent. The tithing is coming in from nearly all the branches, and business moves as busily around the temple as it does around a beehive in May."[5]

Heeding the admonition of peaceful coexistence, the Saints replaced their retaliatory feelings with commitment to finish the city and temple that the Prophet Joseph Smith had envisioned. "We want to build the Temple in this place," said Brigham Young, President of the Twelve, "if we have to build it as the Jews built the walls of the Temple in Jerusalem, with a sword in one hand and the trowel in the other."[6]

"Every man seems determined to do all he can to roll on the work of the Temple as fast as possible," wrote Brigham on another occasion. "There never was a more prosperous time, in general, amongst the saints, since the work commenced. Nauvoo, or, more properly, the 'City of Joseph,' looks like a paradise. . . , Many strangers are pouring in to view the Temple and the city. They express their astonishment and surprise to see the rapid progress of the Temple, and the beauty and grandeur."[7]

But the beauty of the rising Nauvoo Temple exacted a

The picturesque Seventies Hall at sunrise.

heavy toll from the Saints. A guard of four hundred men kept watch "night and day around the Temple," wrote Hosea Stout. "No stranger [was] allowed to come within the square of the Temple Lot."[8] Completing the temple and protecting the builders became the focus of the community. "I do not go out of doors, and look at that house [temple]," wrote Heber C. Kimball, "but the prayer of my heart is 'O, Lord save this people, and help them to build thy house.'"[9]

The Nauvoo Saints struggled with the constant intrusions of neighboring mobs. "Truly, it is trying and grievous," penned Hortensia Merchants, "that we cannot worship God according to the dictates of our own conscience, unmolested."[10] Bathsheba Smith wrote: "Not content with the cruel wrongs inflicted, our persecutors continually annoyed us, but notwithstanding this, rapid progress was made on the Temple and Nauvoo House, until September 1845, when . . . one hundred and seventy five houses belonging to our people in Hancock County [were burned] by the mob. . . . The people who had their houses burned, fled into Nauvoo for shelter. Our house was filled."[11]

As the town grew, the number of laborers multiplied, as did the number of buildings. The Cultural Hall uptown and the Seventies Hall near the river were completed. Brigham Young added two rooms to his house, and Heber C. Kimball and Willard Richards bricked their two-story dwellings. In rapid fashion the city grew

In the Seventies Hall, newly called missionaries practiced preaching before leaving for their assigned fields of labor.

The Wilford Woodruff home was completed in the fall of 1845, just sixty days before he fled from Nauvoo.

by brick and mortar, but the limestone facade of the Nauvoo Temple could not be hurried. In a letter to Wilford Woodruff dated 27 June 1845, Brigham Young wrote, "We have met from time to time to offer up our prayers . . . that the Lord would enable us to finish the Temple . . . that the brethren might obtain their endowments, for this we have supplicated by night and by day."[12]

On 24 May 1845, the years of cooperative labor culminated in the laying of the capstone on the Nauvoo Temple. Of the event it was written: "The singers sang their sweetest notes, and their voices thrilled the hearts of the assemblage; the music of the band, which played on the occasion, never sounded so charming; and when President Young placed the stone in position and said, 'The last stone is now laid upon the temple, and I pray the Almighty, in the name of Jesus, to defend us in this place, and sustain us until the temple is finished and we have all got our endowments.' And all the congregation shouted, 'Hosanna! Hosanna! Hosanna! to God and the Lamb, amen! amen! and amen!' and repeated these words the second and third time, the spirit of God descended upon the people, gladness filled every heart, and tears of joy coursed down many cheeks."[13] George A. Smith concurred, "My feelings were such that I could not suppress a flood of tears."[14]

Brigham Young wrote of the harmony present on that sacred occasion: "The most perfect union, peace and

The Sylvester Stoddard tin shop and home were among many brick structures finished after the death of Joseph Smith.

good feeling has invariably prevailed in our midst and still continues. It seems like a foretaste of celestial enjoyment and Millennial glory."[15]

Before that glory could be realized, however, the Latter-day Saints would become exiles from the United States, fulfilling Joseph Smith's prophecy that "the Saints would continue to suffer much affliction and would be driven to the Rocky Mountains."[16] As the Saints prepared to move to the West, the City of Joseph became "one vast mechanic shop, as nearly every family was engaged in making wagons. Our parlor was used as a paint shop in which to paint wagons," recalled Bathsheba Smith. "All were making preparations to leave [the city] the ensuing winter."[17] Thousands of Saints presented a dichotomy of grand proportions. On the one hand was a scene of determination to complete the Nauvoo Temple, the homes, the shops, and to cultivate the farms. Yet those who built the city simultaneously scurried to construct wagons in which they would transport their families to uncharted regions in the Rocky Mountains, abandoning the holdings they were so diligently improving.

A welcome interlude in preparing for the westward movement was the chance to participate in the ordinances of the temple. Between December 1845 and February 1846, a period of less than ten weeks, more than 5,500 Saints received their endowments in the Nauvoo Temple. Among them was Martha Thomas, who wrote: "We esteemed it a privilege to work on the House of God . . . until it was finished. We were then called to the house to receive the blessings the Lord has in store for the faithful, which amply paid them for all their labors."[18] Brigham Young delayed crossing the Mississippi River until all who wished received these blessings. "I walked some distance from the Temple supposing the crowd would disperse," wrote Brigham, "but on

Reflections of a sunrise shine in a windowpane of the Seventies Hall.

Brigham Young was a cabinet maker by trade, and this upstairs bedroom in his home shows the quality of his work.

returning I found the house filled to overflowing. Looking upon the multitude and knowing their anxiety, as they were thirsting and hungering for the word, we continued at work diligently in the House of the Lord."[19]

Yet the day of departure came quickly. On 4 February 1846, Brigham Young announced: "Brethren awake!— . . . Let every branch in the east, west, north, and south, be determined to flee out of Babylon, either by land or by sea. . . . Judgment is at the door; and it will be easier to go now, than to wait until it comes."[20] He assured the Latter-day Saints of the rightness of leaving the City of Joseph: "We can do almost anything, for our Father in heaven will strengthen us, if we strengthen ourselves. He will work according to our faith. . . . If we say, in the name of the Lord we will go! and set ourselves about it, he will help us."[21]

As the Saints made final preparations to leave, they expressed sorrow. A question for many was a simple "Why?" Parley P. Pratt answered their question: "The great amount of expense and labor we have been at to purchase lands, build houses, the Temple, &c.; we might ask, why is it that we have been at all this outlay and expense, and then are called to leave it? [The Lord] would answer that the people of God always were required to make sacrifices, and if we have a sacrifice to make, he is in favor of its being something worthy of the people of God. We do not want to leave a desolate place, to be a reproach to us but something that will be a monument of our industry and virtue. Our houses, our farms, this Temple and all we leave will be a monument to those who may visit the place of our industry, diligence, and virtue. There is no sacrifice required at the hands of the people of God but shall be rewarded to them an hundred fold, in time or eternity."[22]

To keep their precious things away from the mobbers, some Saints lowered their valuables—like this china displayed in the Wilford Woodruff dining room—into their privies.

In February 1846, in subzero temperatures, the first Saints left Nauvoo for the West. The last building they passed was the Seventies Hall.

Blocks of ice like these clogged the Mississippi River on 4 February 1846 as Charles Shumway crossed the river to Iowa Territory.

THE EXODUS

Overnight the City of Joseph was transformed into a wagon factory. Blacksmiths, carpenters, and wheelwrights were on call day and night. Every available space, from the shop to the parlor, was used to assemble wagon boxes, sew covers, and make wheels. Nearly fifteen hundred wagons were ready for the westward trek by Thanksgiving of 1845, and another two thousand were partially completed by midwinter.

Confident that all wagons would be ready by spring of 1846, Church trustees advertised: "The undersigned wish to purchase one thousand Yoke of Cattle, from four to eight years old for the removal of the Church of Jesus Christ of Latter Day Saints. A ready market will be found [in Nauvoo] for all the working Cattle and Mules that may be brought in."[1] More than "twenty thousand acres of good farming lands, some of which are highly improved" were offered in exchange for "goods, cash, oxen, cows, sheep, wagons, &c."[2]

The preparation time was shortened by threats against the Nauvoo community and its leaders. Governor Thomas Ford of Illinois admitted, "with a view to hasten [the Saints'] removal they were made to believe that the President would order the regular army to Nauvoo as soon as the navigation opened in the spring—to arrest their leaders and prevent the removal."[3] John Taylor, editor of the *Nauvoo Neighbor*, assured the mob element: "We are making all the preparation in our power to leave the United States next spring, because we are compelled by mobocracy. . . . We will suffer wrong rather than do wrong."[4]

The Mormons could not sell their homes, fields, and shops for fair market value before their departure. Aaron Johnson sold his Nauvoo property, valued at $4,000, for $150. Jacob Weiler received only $200 for his $1,200 home. John D. Lee was offered $800 for his $8,000 home. "My fanaticism would not allow me to take that for it," he wrote. "I locked it up, selling only one stove out of it, for which I received eighty yards of cloth. The building with its twenty-seven rooms, I turned over to the committee, to be sold to help the poor away. The committee informed me afterwards that they sold the house for $12.50."[5]

Despite the economic disappointments, Heber C. Kimball declared: "I am glad the time of our Exodus has come; I have looked for it for years. There may be individuals who will look at their pretty houses and gardens and say, 'it is hard to leave them;' but I tell you, when you start, you will put on your knapsacks and follow after us."[6] Parley Pratt said, "The Lord designs to lead us to a wider field of action, where there will be more room for the saints to grow and increase, and where there will be no one to say we crowd them."[7] Eliza R. Snow put similar sentiments into a poem:

> Let us go—let us go
> to the wilds for a home
> Where the wolf and the roe
> and the buffalo roam—
> Where beneath our own vines,
> we in peace, may enjoy
> The fruits of our labors,
> with none to annoy.[8]

President Brigham Young counseled those who hesitated to leave Nauvoo in the winter of 1846: "When a family is called to go, everything necessary may be put into the wagon within four hours, at least, for if we are here many days, our way will be hedged up. Our enemies have resolved to intercept us whenever we start. I

The Brigham Young home in winter, with a horse-drawn sleigh in the foreground.

should like to push on as far as possible before they are aware of our movements."[9]

On 4 February 1846, in nearly zero-degree weather, Charles Shumway loaded his ox-drawn wagon onto a flatboat and became the first to cross the Mississippi River on the now-famous Mormon trek. Others from Nauvoo crossed the river to join Shumway that first day. On flatboats, lighters, and skiffs the Saints formed a makeshift fleet carrying exiles to the Territory of Iowa.

"I was informed nine children were ushered into the world," wrote Eliza R. Snow about an evening on the trek through Iowa Territory. "From that time, as we journeyed, mothers gave birth to offspring under almost every variety of circumstances except those to which they had been accustomed. . . . Let it be remembered that the mothers referred to . . . were not those who, in the woods of nature, nursed their offspring amid reeds and rushes, or in the obscure recesses of rocky caverns."[10]

The exiles faced hardships from the bitter cold of Iowa's wilderness. "I frosted my feet which occasioned me considerable inconvenience for several weeks," noted Eliza R. Snow.[11] "We are leaving our homes today to cross the frozen river," wrote Joseph Young. "We must not look back, but placing our faith in God, we must leave our destiny in His hands. Joseph appears to be cheerful, but the little children cry much of the time. They suffer with the cold, and the fires are cheerless."[12]

In the council room of the Brigham Young home, plans were formulated for the Saints' exodus to the Rocky Mountains.

Yet, in spite of the hardships inherent in the trek, the people chose to abandon their beautiful city. Wilford Woodruff reflected, "I looked upon the Temple and City of Nauvoo as I retired from it and felt to ask the Lord to preserve it as a monument of the sacrifice of his Saints."[13] Brigham Young wrote, "Our homes, gardens, orchards, farms, streets, bridges, mills, public halls, magnificent Temple, and other public improvements we leave as a monument of our patriotism, industry, economy, uprightness of purpose and integrity of heart; and as a living testimony of the falsehood and wickedness of those who charge us with disloyalty to the Constitution of our country, idleness and dishonesty."[14]

Brigham led a body of the Saints across the frozen Mississippi River on 15 February 1846. "Do not think," he wrote, "I hate to leave my house and home. No! far from that. I am so free from bondage at this time that Nauvoo looks like a prison to me. It looks pleasant ahead but dark to look back."[15] Witnessing their departure was young Joseph F. Smith, who noted, "The river froze within a day or two, because of heavy frost, which enabled them to cross as they did, and thus the first real marvel and manifestation of the mercy and the power of God was manifest, in making a roadway across the Mississippi a mile wide at that place by which our people could go on their journey to the West."[16]

The courageous act of crossing the frozen river does not mirror the experiences of the westward-bound

A wagon wheel being made in the Blacksmith and Wainwright Shop.

The cold autumn sky over the Blacksmith and Wainwright Shop suggests the emotions felt 150 years earlier as the Saints made wagons and wheels in preparation to leave Nauvoo.

Covered wagons at the end of Parley Street await the dawn of an icy Nauvoo morning.

pioneer seeking greener pastures in Oregon or of the adventurous "forty-niner" hoping to claim gold in California. The economic motive dominant among other immigrants pales in comparison with the Latter-day Saints' determination to find a safe haven.

The Saints turned their "hearts and all their labours towards the setting sun, for they desire[d] to be so far removed from those who [had] been their oppressors, that there [should] be an everlasting barrier between them and future persecution."[17] As they journeyed through Iowa they were dubbed the Camp of Israel.

Altho' in woods and tents we dwell
Shout, shout, O Camp of Israel
No christian mobs on earth can bind
Our thoughts, or steal our peace of mind.

We've left The City of Nauvoo
And our beloved Temple too,
And to the wilderness we'll go
Amid the winter frosts and snow.

Our homes were dear—we lov'd them well
Beneath our roofs we hop'd to dwell,
And honor the great God's commands
By mutual rights of christian lands.

Our persecutors will not cease
Their murd'rous spoiling of our peace
And have decreed that we must go
To wilds where reeds and rushes grow.

The Camp—the Camp—its numbers swell
Shout, shout O Camp of Israel!
The King the Lord of hosts is near
His armies guard our front and rear.[18]

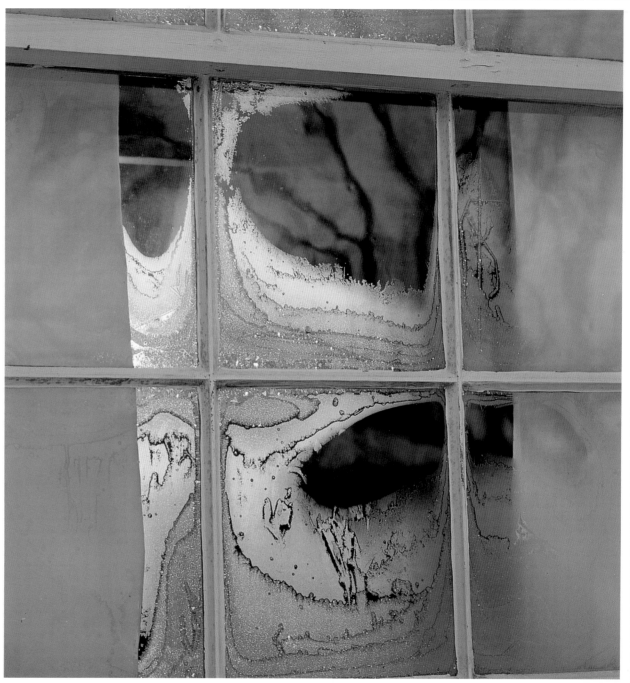

Frost forms on the inside of the windows in the Stoddard home and tin shop as outside temperatures dip to 20 degrees below zero.

A few Saints tarried in Nauvoo, for economic or other reasons. "Spring came in time with all its loveliness and with it also came the mobocrats," wrote Eliza Gibbs. "The city was soon flooded with them, cursing the Mormons and threatening them with extermination. . . . [I] had to get out of Nauvoo the best way I could without any assistance. How I managed, I hardly know, but I was prosperous in my undertakings."[19] Mariah Pulsipher wrote: "We started west in the spring with an old wagon, one yoke of oxen, one cow and all the things we could load in the wagon. We felt to rejoice that we escaped with our lives."[20]

By summer Nauvoo was nearly deserted, and portions of the city had been destroyed. In September 1846 the remaining Saints in Nauvoo faced an infuriated mob that attacked the city, killing some and forcing many to cross the Mississippi River to Iowa. "And, hard as it is to write it—it must ever remain a truth on the page of history—. . . brothers, sisters, fathers, mothers, and children were driven by mob violence from a free and independent State . . . and were compelled to flee from the fire, the sword, the musket, and the cannon's mouth, as from the demon of death . . . while the Temple of the Lord is left solitary in the midst of our enemies, an enduring monument of the diligence and integrity of the Saints."[21]

Joseph F. Smith, the son of martyr Hyrum Smith, remembered the September mobbing: "My mother and her family were compelled to take all that they could move out of the house—their bedding, their clothing, the little food they possessed, leaving the furniture and everything else standing in the house, and fled across the river, where we camped without tent or shelter until the war was over. The city was conquered."[22]

After the attack, Nauvoo's success as a city was forgotten as it

The Heber C. Kimball home was abandoned as the family fled from Nauvoo.

plummeted into obscurity. Thomas L. Kane wrote of his visit to deserted Nauvoo: "It was a natural impulse to visit this inviting region. I procured a skiff, and rowing across the river, landed at the chief wharf of the city. No one met me there. I looked, and saw no one. I could hear no one move; though the quiet everywhere was such that I heard the flies buzz, and the water-ripples break against the shallow of the beach. I walked through the solitary streets. The town lay as in a dream, under some deadening spell of loneliness, from which I almost feared to wake it. For plainly it had not slept long. There was no grass growing up in the paved ways. Rains had not entirely washed away the prints of dusty footsteps.

"Yet I went about unchecked. I went into empty workshops, rope walks, and smithies. The spinner's wheel was idle; the carpenter had gone from his work-bench and shavings, his unfinished sash and casing. Fresh bark was in the tanner's vat, and the fresh-chopped light wood stood piled against the baker's oven. The blacksmith's shop was cold; but his coal heap and lading pool and crooked water horn were all there, as if he had just gone off for a holiday. No work people anywhere looked to know my errand . . .—no one called out to me from any open window, or dog sprang forward to bark an alarm. I could have supposed the people hidden in their houses, but the doors were unfastened; and when at last I timidly entered them, I found dead ashes white

upon the hearths, and had to tread a tiptoe, as if walking down the aisle of a country church, to avoid rousing irreverent echoes from the naked floors."[23]

English journalist Charles Lanman left a historical account of his visit to the abandoned community: "When this city was in its glory, every dwelling was sur-rounded with a garden . . . but now all the fences are in ruin, and lately crowded streets actually rank with vegetation. Of the houses left standing, not more than one out of ten was occupied, excepting by the spider and the toad. Hardly a window retained a full pane of glass, and the doors were broken, and open, and hingeless."[24]

The once-proud city was draped in blight and ruin. Few remained to mourn her loss, for the Latter-day Saints had abandoned their homes and shops in Nauvoo for the valleys of the Rocky Mountains.

Parley Street is nicknamed "Street of Tears" in memory of the sorrow of the exiles as they waited their turn to cross the river and begin the trek west.

A view of Nauvoo across the Mississippi River.

EPILOGUE

For generations the grandeur of Nauvoo lay shrouded in ruins. Nineteenth-century travelers scoffed at assertions that the town of rubble was once a beautiful city, even the pride of the Mississippi Valley. When historian B. H. Roberts visited the community in 1885, he observed, "The whole place has a half-deserted, half-dilapidated appearance, and seems to be withering under a blight, from which it cannot recover."[1] In the collective memory of such visitors, the phrase "Nauvoo the beautiful" was a fanciful exaggeration.

Yet Nauvoo today is beautiful. What transpired to change the rubble of yesteryear to a scene of "singular and most striking beauty"? The story of the rebirth of Nauvoo, the re-creating of a "light of the world—a city set upon a hill" is almost as interesting as the saga of Joseph Smith and the early Saints.[2] It began in 1905 in the old section of historic Nauvoo as nearly a hundred members of The Church of Jesus Christ of Latter-day Saints held a two-day conference. Attending the conference was eighty-six-year-old Lorin Farr of Ogden, Utah, who in earlier years had been one of Nauvoo's founders. "All of the people I talked with [in Nauvoo] were anxious to have our people come back," said Brother Farr. "I told them most of the people that were men and women when we left 60 years ago were not living, but I thought some time in the near future many of the Latter-day Saints would come and assist in the building of a beautiful city."[3] Among those who came were Wilford Wood, Bryant S. Hinckley, and J. LeRoy Kimball. On 19 February 1937 Wilford Wood attempted to purchase the former Nauvoo Temple site from Mr. Anton of Nauvoo. "It seemed as though no agreement could be made as I was limited to the price I could pay. An influence came to me and I said, 'Are you going to try and make me pay an exorbitant price for the blood of a martyred Prophet, when you know this property rightfully belongs to the Mormon people?' I felt the spirit of the Prophet Joseph in that place. Mr. Anton said we will sell the lot for $900.00. I grasped his hand, then the hand of the Cashier of the Bank, and the agreement was made and signed. We parted the best of friends."[4]

In 1938 Bryant S. Hinckley wrote of his confidence that Nauvoo would rise again and would "bring into relief one of the most heroic, dramatic, and fascinating pioneer achievements ever enacted upon American soil. It will reveal a record of fortitude and self-reliance; of patriotic and courageous endeavor, that should stimulate faith in the hearts of all men. . . . Annually thousands . . . will visit it." He prophetically added: "Nauvoo is destined to become one of the most beautiful shrines of America."[5]

Chicago artist Lane K. Newberry stated in 1939: "I feel that the World should honor men and women who accomplished what the Mormons accomplished in Nauvoo—the building of a substantial city in the short period of six years. . . . There was a spirit back of the building of this city that the World needs today, and it only can be attained by honoring those who had it yesterday."[6]

In 1954, when Dr. J. LeRoy Kimball was making his first restoration efforts on the 1840s home of his ancestor Heber C. Kimball, thousands asked to tour the structure. "I really get enthusiastic about the potential of Nauvoo," remarked Dr. Kimball. He envisioned a restored city, a "Williamsburg of the Midwest," with brick homes and trade shops, "and the amazing thing

is," he said, "so do all of the experts."[7] But old-timers in Nauvoo faulted his plan, much like the hecklers of Joseph Smith, who had said, "I told the people I would build up a city and the old inhabitants replied 'We will be damned if you can.'"[8]

Undaunted by opponents, in 1962 LeRoy Kimball and a few others who shared his vision of a renewed community formed Nauvoo Restoration, Inc. The purpose of the corporation was to restore "the historical importance of Old Town Nauvoo as it was when it flourished in 1839–1846 as one of the vibrant forces in the westward expansion of America."[9] Although the purpose appeared an impossible quest, it was within reach of the enthusiastic corporate members.

Thirty years after the foundation meeting of the corporation, historic Nauvoo was recognized as the largest and finest historic preservation in mid-America. The Camera Association, Inc., applauded the restoration with its highest rating: "Everything about the place is first class." The National Park Service named Nauvoo as "a place of exceptional value in our national history."[10] The United States government recognized Nauvoo as a national historic site.

These plaudits did not come without the cooperative labor of archaeologists, historians, visionary financiers, and Church leaders. Summer after summer, archaeologists plied trowels and whisk brooms to remove dirt from artifacts, attempting to preserve the past. They marveled at the caliber of the skilled artisans of earlier years as they ran fingers over smooth stone and broken pottery. Historians guided modern architects, builders, and designers in the restoration and reconstruction of replica homes and shops depicting life in Nauvoo during the early 1840s. Financiers bought land and kept the vision of a restored community alive. Leaders of The Church of Jesus

The Vinson Knight home was restored by Nauvoo Restoration, Inc.

Interior of the Scovil Bakery.

Christ of Latter-day Saints and the Reorganized Church of Jesus Christ of Latter Day Saints worked together to build a shared dream of a beautiful Nauvoo.

Today more than a thousand acres in historic Nauvoo flourish like a manicured city park. Tall trees, native vegetation, period flowers, and medicinal herbs grow amid expansive lawns. Nestled in the park-like atmosphere are the restored historic sites, reminders of beautiful Nauvoo. Hosts in the Scovil Bakery, the Browning Gun Shop, the Mansion House, and Riser's Cheap Boot Store open doors for visitors once again. Carriage rides, craft demonstrations, and theatrical performances tell the saga of old Nauvoo.

A city has been reborn as a monument to Joseph Smith and those who once walked the streets of Nauvoo. But its light is only a small reflection of what the Prophet began so many years ago. The Book of Mormon, which in 1840 was published only in the English language, is now translated and published in its entirety in more than fifty languages, with selections from the book available in another forty-six dialects. Temples like the Nauvoo Temple that required the tithe of one day in ten have been built in countries throughout the world. Mormonism did not die in Nauvoo with the martyrdom of Joseph Smith or the exodus of Saints from the city. Unlike the once beautiful city of Nauvoo, which suffered from neglect and blight for decades, The Church of Jesus Christ of Latter-day Saints has continued to project as a beacon of light to the world.

We express our gratitude to Joseph Smith and the Saints who built the city of Nauvoo. For their accomplishments, sacrifices, and courage, we give thanks.

Stately trees lend grandeur to historic Nauvoo. The Sarah Granger Kimball home is seen in the background.

NOTES

PROLOGUE

1. Joseph Smith–History 1:17.
2. Joseph Smith–History 1:25.
3. Joseph Smith–History 1:34.
4. William W. Phelps, in *Latter Day Saints' Messenger and Advocate* 1 (September 1835): 177–79.
5. Beatrice Cannon Evans and Jonathan Russel Cannon, eds., *Cannon Family Historical Treasury* (Salt Lake City: George Cannon Family Association, 1967), 35.
6. Joseph Smith, *Teachings of the Prophet Joseph Smith*, sel. Joseph Fielding Smith (Salt Lake City: Deseret Book, 1938), 139.
7. Lucy Mack Smith, *History of Joseph Smith by His Mother*, ed. Preston Nibley (Salt Lake City: Bookcraft, 1958), 185.
8. Ibid., 215–16.
9. Joseph Smith, *History of the Church of Jesus Christ of Latter-day Saints*, 7 vols., ed. B. H. Roberts (Salt Lake City: Deseret Book, 1976), 4:46n. Hereafter cited as *History of the Church*.
10. Parley P. Pratt, *Autobiography of Parley P. Pratt*, ed. Parley P. Pratt, Jr. (Salt Lake City: Deseret Book, 1985), 278.
11. *History of the Church*, 4:370.
12. Ebenezer Robinson, *The Return* 2 (1890): 243. LDS Church Archives.
13. *History of the Church*, 3:268.
14. Orson F. Whitney, *Life of Heber C. Kimball* (Salt Lake City: Bookcraft, 1975), 256.
15. Autobiography of Sarah D. Rich, 1:57; as cited in Leonard J. Arrington, *Charles C. Rich* (Provo, Utah: Brigham Young University Press, 1974), 69.
16. Quoted by Stanley B. Kimball, "Nauvoo," *Improvement Era* 65 (July 1962): 548.
17. Jane Robinson Hindly, "Jane C. Robinson Hindly Reminiscences and Diary," as cited in Richard Neitzel Holzapfel and Jeni Broberg Holzapfel, *Women of Nauvoo* (Salt Lake City: Bookcraft, 1992), 14–15.
18. Jane Manning James, "Biography of Jane Elizabeth Manning James," LDS Church Archives.
19. *History of the Church*, 6:165–66.
20. B. H. Roberts, *A Comprehensive History of The Church of Jesus Christ of Latter-day Saints*, 6 vols. (Provo, Utah: Brigham Young University Press, 1965), 2:349–50. Hereafter cited as *Comprehensive History of the Church*.

A WILDERNESS

1. *Comprehensive History of the Church*, 2:7–8.
2. *History of the Church*, 3:375.
3. *Comprehensive History of the Church*, 2:9.
4. *History of the Church*, 3:375.
5. Quoted in Matthias F.

Cowley, *Wilford Woodruff, History of His Life and Labors* (Salt Lake City: Bookcraft, 1975), 104.
6. Elizabeth Ann Whitney, "A Leaf From an Autobiography," *Woman's Exponent* 7 (15 November 1878): 91.
7. Maureen Ursenbach Beecher, ed., "All Things Move in Order in the City: The Nauvoo Diary of Zina Diantha Huntington Jacobs," *BYU Studies* 19 (Spring 1979): 317.
8. George Peck, *The Life and Times of Rev. George Peck, D.D., written by himself* (New York: Nelson and Phillips, 1874), 201–2. Photostatic copy in Family Lands and Records Center, Nauvoo Visitors Center, Nauvoo, IL.
9. Heber J. Grant, in Conference Report, April 1900, 21.
10. Cowley, *Wilford Woodruff*, 109.
11. Orson F. Whitney, *Life of Heber C. Kimball* (Salt Lake City: Bookcraft, 1967), 265–66.
12. Benjamin Brown, *Testimonies for the Truth* (1853) 12, in "LDS Collectors Library," Infobases, 1995 edition.
13. "Lorenzo Brown Journal," 9–10, in "LDS Collectors Library."
14. Mosiah Hancock Autobiography, 20, in "LDS Collectors Library."
15. Lucy Mack Smith, *History of Joseph Smith by His Mother*, edited by Preston Nibley (Salt Lake City: Bookcraft, 1958), 309.

16. *History of the Church*, 5:232.
17. William Mulder and A. Russell Mortensen, *Among the Mormons* (New York: Alfred A. Knopf, 1958), 129.
18. George A. Smith, in *Journal of Discourses*, 26 vols. (London: Latter-day Saints' Book Depot, 1856–86), 13:115.
19. *History of the Church*, 4:133.
20. Richard Neitzel Holzapfel and T. Jeffery Cottle, *Old Mormon Nauvoo and Southeastern Iowa: Historic Photographs and Guide* (Santa Ana, California: Fieldbrook Productions, 1991), 25.
21. Abigail Pitkin to Rebecca Raymond, LDS Church Archives, as quoted in E. Cecil McGavin, *Nauvoo, the Beautiful* (Salt Lake City: Bookcraft, 1972), 41–42.
22. *Comprehensive History of the Church*, 2:84.
23. *Journal of Discourses*, 13:115.

A CITY BY THE MISSISSIPPI

1. Eliza Gibbs Autobiography, typescript, 4, in "LDS Collectors Library," Infobases, 1995 edition.
2. Harvey Cluff Autobiography, typescript, 4–5, in BYU Special Collections, Harold B. Lee Library.
3. John L. Butler Autobiography, 23, in "LDS Collectors Library."
4. Richard Neitzel Holzapfel

and Jeni Broberg Holzapfel, *Women of Nauvoo* (Salt Lake City: Bookcraft, 1992), 34, 52–53.
5. Butler, Autobiography, 23.
6. Quoted in Edward F. Parry, comp., *Stories about Joseph Smith the Prophet* (Salt Lake City: Deseret News Press, 1934), 34–35, as cited in Holzapfel, *Women of Nauvoo*, 34.
7. Mary K. Stout, "From a Nauvoo Pantry," *New Era* 3 (December 1973): 43.
8. *History of the Church*, 6:24.
9. *Comprehensive History of the Church*, 2:351.
10. *History of the Church*, 6:33.
11. Hyrum L. Andrus and Helen Mae Andrus, *They Knew the Prophet* (Salt Lake City: Bookcraft, 1974), 145.
12. E. Cecil McGavin, *Nauvoo, the Beautiful* (Salt Lake City: Bookcraft, 1972), 85–86.
13. Nauvoo Restoration, Inc., script: Brigham Young Journal, 2 September 1841; 31 May 1843.
14. Nauvoo Restoration, Inc., script: Heber C. Kimball Journal, 8 November 1845.
15. Nauvoo Restoration, Inc., script: Wilford Woodruff Journal, 3–4 May 1844.
16. Matthias F. Cowley, *Wilford Woodruff, History of His Life and Labors* (Salt Lake City: Bookcraft, 1975), 159.
17. Nauvoo Restoration, Inc., script: Lyon Drugstore.
18. Nauvoo Restoration, Inc., script: *Nauvoo Neighbor*, 27 December 1843. Some sources say "one to twenty-five cents."

19. Nauvoo Restoration, Inc., script: Lyon Drugstore.
20. T. Edgar Lyon, "The Account Books of the Amos Davis Store at Commerce, Illinois," *BYU Studies* 19 (Winter 1979): 241–43.
21. *Nauvoo Neighbor*, 12 July 1843.
22. Ibid., 24 January 1844.
23. Letter of Ann H. Pitchforth to her parents, 23 April 1845, as cited in Holzapfel, *Women of Nauvoo*, 33.
24. *Times and Seasons*, 1 August 1844.

METROPOLITAN NAUVOO

1. Nauvoo Restoration, Inc., script: Lyon Drugstore; *Nauvoo Neighbor*.
2. Ibid.
3. *History of the Church*, 5:57.
4. Charles Hales Autobiography, typescript, 36, in "LDS Collectors Library," Infobases, 1995 edition.
5. *Nauvoo Neighbor*, 30 October 1844.
6. *Comprehensive History of the Church*, 3:298.
7. Orson Hyde, "Self Government—Constitution of the United States—Church Government, etc.," in *Journal of Discourses*, 6:150.
8. *Times and Seasons*, 15 October 1844.
9. Harvey Cluff Autobiography, typescript, 5, in BYU Special

Collections, Harold B. Lee Library.

10. Orson F. Whitney, *Life of Heber C. Kimball* (Salt Lake City: Bookcraft, 1975), 313.

11. Charles Metten, "Drama," in *Encyclopedia of Mormonism*, 5 vols., ed. Daniel H. Ludlow (New York: Macmillan Publishing Company, 1992), 1:429.

12. Richard Neitzel Holzapfel and Jeni Broberg Holzapfel, *Women of Nauvoo* (Salt Lake City: Bookcraft, 1992), 66.

13. Reta Latimer Halford, "Nauvoo—the City Beautiful" (master's thesis, University of Utah, 1945), 176.

14. Holzapfel, *Women of Nauvoo,* 69.

15. Hosea Stout Diary (1845), typescript, 2:20, in BYU Special Collections, Harold B. Lee Library.

16. *History of the Church,* 5:252.

17. *History of the Church,* 6:134–35.

18. Article of Faith 13.

THE NAUVOO TEMPLE

1. J. Earl Arrington, "William Weeks, Architect of the Nauvoo Temple," *BYU Studies* 9 (Spring 1979): 343.

2. Ibid., 341.

3. Ibid., 346.

4. T. Edgar Lyon, "Recollections of 'Old Nauvooers' Memories from Oral History," *BYU Studies* 18 (Winter 1978): 147–48.

5. Luman Shurtliff Autobiography, typescript, 52–53, in BYU Special Collections, Harold B. Lee Library.

6. *History of the Church,* 5:58.

7. Joseph F. Smith, in Conference Report, October 1917, 8.

8. Maureen Ursenbach, "Eliza

R. Snow's Journal," *BYU Studies* 15 (Summer 1975): 405–6.

9. Drusilla Hendricks, "Reminiscence," as cited in *Nauvoo Neighbor,* 29 October 1845.

10. Hyrum L. Andrus and Helen Mae Andrus, *They Knew the Prophet* (Salt Lake City: Bookcraft, 1974), 130.

11. Wandle Mace Autobiography, typescript, 94, in BYU Special Collections, Harold B. Lee Library.

12. W. W. Phelps, "Temple of God at Nauvoo," *Times and Seasons* 4:830.

13. Mace, Autobiography, 101–2.

14. Brigham Young, in *Journal of Discourses,* 8:228.

15. B. H. Roberts, *Outlines of Ecclesiastical History,* 3rd ed. (Salt Lake City: Deseret News, 1902), 394.

16. Mace, Autobiography, 101–2.

17. *History of the Church,* 6:58.

18. Mace, Autobiography, 94–95.

19. E. Cecil McGavin, *Nauvoo, the Beautiful* (Salt Lake City: Bookcraft, 1972), 89.

20. Josiah Quincy, as quoted in McGavin, *Nauvoo, the Beautiful,* 88.

21. *History of the Church,* 7:434.

THE MARTYRDOM

1. Quoted in Roger D. Launius, "Anti-Mormonism in Illinois: Thomas C. Sharp's Unfinished History of the Mormon War, 1845," *Journal of Mormon History* 15 (1989): 30.

2. *Warsaw Signal,* 29 May 1844.

3. *History of the Church,* 5:259; 6:450.

4. *History of the Church,* 6:549.

5. *History of the Church,* 6:554, 601.

6. *History of the Church,* 6:592.

7. Doctrine and Covenants 135:1.

8. Ibid.

9. Ibid.

10. Ronald K. Esplin, "Life in Nauvoo, June 1884: Vilate Kimball's Martyrdom Letters," *BYU Studies* 19 (Winter 1979): 238.

11. Eliza R. Snow, *Biography and Family Record of Lorenzo Snow, One of the Twelve Apostles of the Church of Jesus Christ of Latter-day Saints* (Salt Lake City: Deseret News, 1884), 80–82.

12. William G. Hartley, "*They are My Friends,*" A History of the Joseph Knight Family 1825–1850 (Provo, Utah: Grandin Book Company, 1986), 153–54.

13. Esplin, "Life in Nauvoo," 238.

14. *New York Herald,* 8 July 1844.

15. *History of the Church,* 7:37.

16. *History of the Church,* 7:198.

THE CITY OF JOSEPH

1. *History of the Church,* 7:398.

2. "Early This Spring We Leave Nauvoo," as quoted in Richard Neitzel Holzapfel and Jeni Broberg Holzapfel, *Women of Nauvoo* (Salt Lake City: Bookcraft, 1992), 143–44.

3. Walter Dean Bowen, "The Versatile W. W. Phelps—Mormon Writer, Educator, and Pioneer" (master's thesis, Brigham Young University, August 1958), 121.

4. *History of the Church,* 7:238.

5. *Millennial Star,* 5 May 1845, 198.

6. *History of the Church,* 7:256.

7. James R. Clark, comp., *Messages of the First Presidency,* 6 vols. (Salt Lake City: Bookcraft, 1965–75), 1:274.

8. Juanita Brooks, ed., *On the Mormon Frontier: The Diary of Hosea Stout, 1844–1861,* 2 vols.

(Salt Lake City: University of Utah Press, 1964), 1:64.

9. *Times and Seasons* 6:987–88.

10. Letter from Hortensia Merchants to William Patrick, 10 July 1844, as quoted in Holzapfel, *Women of Nauvoo,* 132.

11. Bathsheba Smith, Autobiography, typescript, 10–11, in BYU Archives, Harold B. Lee Library.

12. Letter from Brigham Young to Wilford Woodruff in England, 27 June 1845, as quoted in Clark, *Messages,* 1:272.

13. Helen Whitney, "Scenes in Nauvoo," *Woman's Exponent* 11 (1882): 169–70.

14. Merlo J. Pusey, *Builders of the Kingdom, George A. Smith, John Henry Smith, George Albert Smith* (Provo, Utah: BYU Press, 1981), 56.

15. Young to Woodruff, as quoted in Clark, *Messages,* 1:272.

16. *History of the Church,* 5:85.

17. Bathsheba Smith, Autobiography, 12.

18. Mary Thomas, Autobiography, typescript, in BYU Special Collections, Harold B. Lee Library, as quoted in Holzapfel, *Women of Nauvoo,* 159.

19. *History of the Church,* 7:579.

20. *History of the Church,* 7:516.

21. *History of the Church,* 7:517.

22. Clark, *Messages,* 1:283.

THE EXODUS

1. "Notice," *Nauvoo New Citizen,* 10 April 1846, as quoted in Janath R. Cannon, *Nauvoo Panorama: Views of Nauvoo before, during, and after Its Rise, Fall, and Restoration* (Nauvoo, Illinois: Nauvoo Restoration, Inc., 1991), 45.

2. "Farming Lands For Sale,"

Nauvoo New Citizen, as quoted in Cannon, *Nauvoo Panorama,* 47.

3. Governor Thomas Ford, *A History of Illinois from Its Commencement as a State in 1818 to 1847,* 2 vols. (Chicago: Lakeside Press, 1945), 1:413.

4. John Taylor, *Nauvoo Neighbor,* 29 October 1845.

5. Erastus Snow Journal, as quoted in Andrew Karl Larsen, *Erastus Snow: The Life of a Missionary and Pioneer for the Early Mormon Church* (Salt Lake City: University of Utah Press, 1971), 102.

6. *Times and Seasons,* 1 November 1845.

7. *History of the Church,* 7:464.

8. Eliza R. Snow Diary, 28 February 1846, in Eliza R. Snow Collection, LDS Church Archives.

9. *History of the Church,* 7:578.

10. *Comprehensive History of the Church,* 3:45.

11. Eliza R. Snow Diary, February 1846.

12. Dean C. Jessee, "Brigham Young's Family: The Wilderness Years," *BYU Studies* 19 (Summer 1979): 483.

13. Scott G. Kenney, ed., *Wilford Woodruff's Journal: 1833–1898,* 9 vols. (Midvale, Utah: Signature Books, 1983), 3:49.

14. *History of the Church,* 7:603.

15. Jessee, "Brigham Young's Family," 483.

16. Joseph Fielding Smith, *Gospel Doctrine: Selections from the Sermons and Writings of Joseph F. Smith,* 5th ed. (Salt Lake City: Deseret Book, 1939), 499.

17. James R. Clark, comp., *Messages of the First Presidency,* 6 vols. (Salt Lake City: Bookcraft, 1965–75), 1:328.

18. Eliza R. Snow Diary, 19 February 1846.

19. Eliza Gibbs Autobiography,

typescript, 5, in "LDS Collectors Library," Infobases, 1995 edition.

20. Mariah Pulsipher, Autobiography, typescript, BYU Special Collections, Harold B. Lee Library.

21. Clark, *Messages,* 1:325.

22. Smith, *Gospel Doctrine,* 500.

23. Thomas L. Kane, *The Mormons: A Discourse Delivered before The Historical Society of Pennsylvania: March 26, 1950* (Philadelphia: King & Baird, 1850), 3–5.

24. Quoted in E. Cecil McGavin, *The Nauvoo Temple* (Salt Lake City: Deseret Book, 1962), 121.

EPILOGUE

1. *Comprehensive History of the Church,* 3:24.

2. Heber J. Grant, in Conference Report, April 1900, 21.

3. T. Earl Pardoe, *Lorin Farr, Pioneer* (Provo, Utah: Brigham Young University Press, 1953), 305.

4. Wilford Wood Journal, 19 February 1937, typescript, unpaged; photocopy in Family Lands and Records Center, Nauvoo Visitors Center, Nauvoo, Illinois.

5. Quoted in Bryant S. Hinckley, "The Nauvoo Memorial," *Improvement Era,* August 1938, 511.

6. Ibid., 460.

7. "Nauvoo Restoration," *Improvement Era,* July 1967, 18.

8. *History of the Church,* 5:232.

9. For a summary of Nauvoo Restoration, Inc., accomplishments, see T. Edgar Lyon, "The Current Restoration in Nauvoo, Illinois," *Dialogue* 5 (Spring 1970): 12–25.

10. Nauvoo Restoration, Inc., Family Land and Records Center Files, Nauvoo, Illinois.

INDEX